THE GOOD SHEPHERD AND THE CHILD

AND THE CHILD

A JOYFUL JOURNEY

THE GOOD SHEPHERD AND THE CHILD

A JOYFUL JOURNEY

Sofia Cavalletti
Patricia Coulter
Gianna Gobbi
Silvana Quattrocchi Montanaro, M.D.

LITURGY TRAINING PUBLICATIONS

Permission for publication is granted by Most Reverend Aloysius Ambrozic, Archbishop of Toronto; March 16, 1993.

Illustrations by Julie Coulter-English. Designed and typeset by Sally Ann Zegarelli. Cover Design by JP Graphics, Bedford Hills, New York. Printed by D.B. Hess Company, Woodstock, Illinois.

Library of Congress Cataloging-in-Publication Data
The good shepherd and the child: a joyful journey / Sofia Cavaletti
    ...[et al.].
    Previously published: New Rochelle, NY: D. Bosco Multimedia.
c 1994.
    ISBN 1-56854-157-0
    1. Children--Religious Life   2.Church work with children--Catholic Church.
BX2371.G63   1996
268'.432--dc20   96-9874
                                                                       CIP

GSHEP

DEDICATION

"Arise, shine forth..." (Isaiah 60:1)

To my mother and father, and all those who help children in their relationship with God.

ACKNOWLEDGMENTS

Excerpts from the Lectionary, *Sundays and Solemnities*, copyright © Concacan Inc., 1992. Used by permission of the Canadian Conference of Catholic Bishops, Ottawa. The Scripture quotations contained herein are from the *New Revised Standard Version* of the Bible, copyrighted, 1989 by the Division of Christian Education of the National Council of the Churches of Christ in the United States of America. All rights reserved. Excerpts from *Catechesi Tradendae* are taken from *On Catechesis In Our Time*, copyright © 1980 Libreria Editrice Vaticana, Vatican City.

Reference was made in this text to *"Lumen Gentium"* from the "Dogmatic Constitution On the Church", *Vatican Council II: The Conciliar and Post Conciliar Documents,* Austin Flannery, O.P., editor (Costello Publishing Company, New York, 1975), to *Familiaris Consortio in The Role of the Christian Family In The Modern World* (St. Paul Books and Media, Boston), and to *The Religious Potential of the Child* by Sofia Cavalletti. (Trans. by Patricia Coulter and Julie M. Coulter.) Chicago: *Liturgy Training Publications*, 1992.

We are grateful to the many children who, with their silent guidance, have enabled us to write these pages. We are united to parents, catechists and educators in thanking God, who has set us on the path of serving life in its most delicate expression: the child. And we are united with you in asking the help and inspiration of the Spirit of God in the work we share in common.

Among the many who have contributed to bringing this book to print, too numerous to name here, we make grateful mention of only a few: Most Reverend Aloysius Ambrozic, Archbishop of Toronto; Mrs. Julie Coulter-English and my family; Most Reverend Marcel Gervais, Archbishop of Ottawa; Mrs. Helene Royes, Director, and Mrs. Brenda Voisin, Secretary of the Catholic Office of Religious Education; Sister Barbara Olga Warnke, I.B.V.M.; the Sisters of Loretto; and the Sisters of St. Joseph.

To all those involved in the Catechesis of the Good Shepherd who have assisted us in the lengthy process of writing this work (they know who they are!), may this book be the sign of our gratitude to you.

P.C.
Feast of the Presentation of the Lord, 1993
Toronto

CONTENTS

CONTENTS

FOREWORD

The catechesis presented in this book asks us to learn from children, to be guided by them and to provide for their needs. Parents, teachers, and volunteers are challenged to "Become as little children."

The "Catechesis of the Good Shepherd" is led by the child. It is no wonder that it suits all children. No matter what their background, no matter what their culture, this approach has discovered the common needs in all young children. The sick and the disadvantaged and those who are well, all profit from it. It is universal in Africa, Mexico, Canada, the United States, Europe. Children absorb the Catechesis joyfully.

This catechesis is also led by the sound teaching of the Church's tradition. Sacred Scripture, the Liturgy, the Magisterium are all used to reveal the Good News to little children. What a rich storehouse to draw from to delight the child! If you have any interest in the religious formation of young children in the Catholic tradition, reading this book will be for you a truly "joyful journey."

✠ Archbishop Marcel A. Gervais, Ottawa, Canada

INTRODUCTION

"Then I will go...
To God my exceeding joy"—Psalm 43:4

This book is a series of practical reflections and basic suggestions for helping the child's growth as a whole and happy person. It is intended particularly for those who accompany young children on their spiritual journey:

- you parents who help your children take their first and most formative steps on their journey;

- you teachers who care for children during their important years in nursery or preschool settings;

- you catechists who make parish and school into communities where the child's religious potential can flourish;

- and all whose lives are linked to children in a variety of ways, from grandparents and godparents to pastors and religious educators.

This book is also for those who want to experience more deeply God's loving presence in the "bits and pieces," as the Irish poet says, of our everyday lives.

INITIATION INTO LOVE

Our theme is God's covenant with young children and a way of being with children that helps them to live their relationship with God. It is a book about initiating children into that covenant relationship, helping children to receive and respond to God's unconditional, personal, love for each of them: "I have called you by name, you are mine....Because you are precious in my sight, and honored, and I love you" (Isaiah 43:1, 4).

God's covenant relationship with each of us is the central theme of the Bible. In the covenant relationship with God, it is God who loves us first (1 John 4:19), even from the time before our birth (Psalm 139:13). Throughout our life God supports and carries us tenderly (Isaiah 46: 3-4) with a love that will never change nor end (Jeremiah 31:3).

The covenant relationship is the core of the Christian message. Jesus takes the first step and comes to each of us so that we may have life to the full (John 10:10) and to give us joy in our love together (John 15:11).

The love and joy in living the covenant is meant for everyone, including children. At the Christmas liturgy, the Gospel message is called the "Good news and great joy to all the world." Also, the Christmas Mass ends with this solemn blessing: "God sent his angels to shepherds to herald the great joy of our Savior's birth. May he fill you with joy and make you heralds of his gospel."

THE WHOLE MESSAGE
FOR THE CHILD

In responding to this call, we are invited to tell the "whole" message (Acts 5:20). If we are addressing the Good News to the child, a person who is an unity of many different parts, we need to speak to the whole child as well.

The whole message for the whole child, this is our focus. Although they are interwoven, Part One of the book will be about God and the child primarily, the *who* and the *why*. Part Two will deal concretely with the message, the *what* and the *how*.

There is a risk in taking this approach. It may mean your questions are not answered as completely as you might wish. However we chose this holistic approach in an attempt to avoid the greater risk of dividing the child's life into "compartments"—home, parish, school, or separating the child's development into distinct parts—physical, intellectual, affective, social, and religious.

Home, school and parish are all parts of the child's life. The child's growth includes all the aspects of body and mind, heart and spirit. Whatever our own unique role is in relation to the child, all of us are involved in the child's life.

What we hope to do in this book is to provide an approach to the child as an unified person and to welcome you into our conversation so that all together we can help the child's journey with God.

The invitation to join our conversation is meant quite literally, since this book began that way. A group of friends, with different expertise, meeting in the family room of a home, and trying to respond to the questions put to us by two Canadian bishops: "What would you say to a mother of six children? to a kindergarten teacher? to a catechist in a parish?" The book took shape in what was to become a sort of on-going long distance conversation, sometimes in speaking, other times by writing. While it was unfolding you were the focus, as if you were there with us and together we were exchanging experiences and insights in a simple conversational way.

COVENANT RELATIONSHIP

Part One, composed of three chapters, is a dialogue among three long-time collaborators in the field of the religious formation of children. All three chapters concentrate on the young child and each voice brings a different area of specialization to the discussion.

Dr. Sofia Cavalletti opens the conversation by facing directly some of the most difficult questions in terms of early childhood religious education:

- Do young children need religious education?
- Do young children have the capacity to live the relationship with God?
- Is it important for their growth as whole persons?
- If so, when and what and how do we tell them about God's covenant of love with them?

She continues to address questions like these in Part Two, but in this first chapter her response is essentially a personal account. Although her extensive biblical scholarship gives a solid basis for her reflections, they are not offered on the level of theory. Rather, Sofia seeks for answers in the light of her forty years' experience with children.

As well as this, she draws on the combined experience of a wide-ranging network of colleagues from a variety of countries and cultures. Chapter One is a statement, warm with gratitude, of what young children have helped her to see both about God and themselves. About God: God's power to touch and satisfy the deep, vital needs in young children and to give growth to their great inner potential. About children: their tremendous capacity—in her words—

to fall in love and be in love with God in a manner that creates harmony and happiness within them, with others and with their world.

This opening chapter sets the tone for what is to follow in Part Two, where we continue to address core issues in a practical, concrete way.

PARENTS: "ORIGINAL AND IRREPLACEABLE"

Chapter Two contains Dr. Silvana Montanaro's contribution. It centers on the very beginnings of the child's life from before birth and on through the first three years. While Silvana's medical training provides a specialized scientific background for this chapter, it is not written from a merely clinical perspective. Instead, Silvana is meeting with parents and teachers on common ground, speaking warmly about experiences she shares with them as mother, grandmother and educator.

Three important factors are implied in her down-to-earth insights. First, Silvana's discussion is rooted in the context of the family. This emphasis is clearly a statement about the value of the family, the primary community in the faith journey of the child, the "domestic Church," as the Second Vatican Council regards it (*Dogmatic Constitution on the Church*, Chapter 2, No. 11).

Just as significant is the respect with which Dr. Montanaro addresses parents and all those who care for very young children. Every action a parent does to or with the child, however mundane it may seem, is truly education. All that a parent *is* becomes a powerful influence in the child's present and future formation. Parenting is a ministry or "service to life," as Silvana calls it. In her view, each parent has the dignity of being the "original and irreplaceable" person in the child's religious journey (*The Role of the Christian Family in the Modern World*, No. 53).

Third, you will notice that Silvana's references to religious education appear few in proportion to her suggestions for helping the child's psycho-physical and social development. Her conviction that every aspect of the child's growth can and must be considered crucial to the child's growth in faith rests on the belief that the glory of God is a child fully alive, fully human (to make a variation on Irenaeus' insight). Or, to use St. Thomas Aquinas' phrase, Silvana's incarnational orientation implies that "grace builds on nature."

HERALDS OF JOY

Chapter Three, by Professor Gianna Gobbi, picks up the thread and carries it forward into the later period of early childhood. Gianna, who directs the training courses for "Assistants to Infancy" with Silvana Montanaro, offers guidance for creating a nurturing faith environment, from the newborn stage up to and through school-starting time.

Gianna has boundless confidence in the abilities of child and adult alike. This is reflected, for instance, in her encouraging advice to parents, teachers, and catechists: *you* are the child's principal resource; what you already have in your environment can be easily adapted to provide rich possibilities for the child's growth.

The frontiers of the family are extended to include the school and parish settings. Gianna was a co-worker with Maria Montessori (Italy's first woman physician and founder of an educational method) and an educator of young children. This accounts for her appreciation of the teaching vocation and easily adaptable suggestions for the classroom situation.

Chapter Two also reflects Professor Gobbi's other specialty, catechesis with children. In 1954 she co-founded the Center of Catechesis in Rome for children with Sofia Cavalletti. A few years later this also became the site of what is now an internationally recognized training Center for adults as well. To Gianna is due in large measure the design and preparation of an unique environment and materials to facilitate and foster the child's relationship with God.

Week in, week out since that time, Gianna, like Sofia, has had direct contact with children. This wealth of experience is distilled into two guiding points applicable to home, school and parish:

- preparing a special environment for children (referred to as "atrium," a recall to the place in the early Christian basilica where the first Christians received their formation in the faith);

- preparing special tools for the child, which she calls *materials* (referring to the models—wooden, paper, etc.—that serve as means for the child's encounter with God and are designed to nourish the child's meditative spirit).

These are the two pivotal points on which Gianna's practical discussion of the catechetical themes rotate. This leads into the detailed treatment of these themes, which is the subject of the second section of this work.

LIFE IN ABUNDANCE

Part Two begins our in-depth treatment of specific catechetical topics for children. Generally, this section focuses on themes from the bible and liturgy. Chapters Five through Seven, and Ten, discuss scriptural themes, especially the Good Shepherd parable, and parables of the kingdom, and the accounts of Christ's birth and resurrection. Chapters Eight and Nine deal with liturgical themes, including suggestions for introducing children to Baptism and the Eucharist, two of the sacraments of initiation. The following points offer some background to assist you in your reading of this section.

- While Part Two is dedicated to discussing the core themes of the Christian message and how they are presented to young children, it is *not* limited only to young children.

A few examples will illustrate the possible applications of Part Two's presentations: they have been used as the basis of parish and school programs for children preparing to celebrate the sacraments of First Eucharist and Reconciliation, and as the key concepts in adult formation courses. After one such course, a woman who is a mother of two children and high school teacher as well, commented: "This has reawakened my relationship with God." This is not an isolated instance. Another example involves a university professor. Once, when he wanted to convey the essence of the Eucharistic mystery to his post-graduate theology students, he used what is virtually the same presentation contained here on the Mass, including the materials (Chapter Nine).

This is mentioned by way of indicating that the themes presented in Part Two (outlined systematically in the *Appendix*) represent the heart of the Christian mystery. They have proven to satisfy the deep hunger in young children—the "littlest" need the "greatest," as Sofia maintains—but they are also applicable to more than the young child.

- In Part Two we try to respond to those who repeatedly ask us, "But how do I do it with children?" For this reason we have offered a rather detailed outline, in schematic format, of the essential themes as we present them to children. We do so with some trepidation, since "the Word of God is living and active" (Hebrews 4:12) and cannot be confined within the limits of any presentation or lesson plan. You are encouraged to read what we have written in this spirit.

The final chapters, on prayer and the child's moral life, return to the theme of the covenant relationship. Love giving, love responding; this is the child's joy. And ours, because in sharing the child's spiritual journey we discover that the face of love God turns towards the child is the same that is looking at us.

In closing, here is a true story of a young boy, whose mother related this experience. At the time it occurred, her son was three years old.

With their four children, she and her husband, when his firefighter's shift permitted, would gather in the evening for a little quiet time and prayer. What is interesting about this story, as the mother tells it, is that she did not have any great expectations about their prayer time, especially in the case of her son Mark. She admitted to questioning herself as to what, if anything, he was getting out of these moments. In fact, she tended to think that his real interest was in being allowed to light the candle at the start and snuff it out at the end—an activity his father otherwise did not encourage!

For the few previous evenings the family had been speaking together about the Good Shepherd. The older children joined in, relishing how the Good Shepherd knows and calls them by name. But Mark said nothing.

Afterwards the children went to bed. Following their familiar routine, as she tucked them in, the mother would exchange a few words with each of her children. When she was settling Mark into bed, she whispered to him, "The Good Shepherd loves you and he calls you by your name." "No he doesn't," Mark replied.

Not knowing what to say to this, the mother stayed silent. Then Mark spoke again. "He doesn't call me Mark. He calls me 'Joy'."

In relating this, his mother added, "He was so small. I don't know where the word 'joy' came from. He never used it before." Now, six years later, that moment still has an impact on her. Retelling it seems to deepen her own joy.

PART ONE

Sofia Cavalletti
Silvana Quattrocchi Montanaro, M.D.
Gianna Gobbi

1. GOD AND THE CHILD TOGETHER

Sofia Cavalletti

From what has been said in the Introduction it is obvious that young children under six are rich in potential, and that the education we provide is a very valuable contribution to their growth during these years and later in life. Is this also true in the case of young children's religious potential? Does religious education during these early years contribute positively to their growth?

WHY RELIGIOUS EDUCATION?

I want to begin by spending some time reflecting with you about these questions and others like them which come to mind. Perhaps they are yours as well or have been put to you by others:

- Do young children have the capacity to live in relationship with God?
- Does religious education respond to a vital need in the child's spirit? Is it something they are asking of us?
- Or is it only something we value and therefore impose on children?
- Does the absence of some form of religious formation affect the young child's harmonious development or not?
- Does religion enrich or complicate their life?

I want to describe the two ways we have searched for answers to these questions.

THE CHILD'S OWN RESPONSE

The first way was to see whether or not young children demonstrate the capacity to be in relationship with God, even when they do not receive religious instruction. This is not easy, because it demands great attentiveness to see manifestation of certain potentials of the human spirit. Over the years we have been documenting incidents involving young children from very different families and cultures who did not receive any special attention in the area of religious formation.[1] Here is one example.

> A little three and a half year old girl asked her father where the world came from. Her father, who is not a believer, gave her a long speech to explain that the world had not been created, and so on. After this explanation he added that some people say that everything was made by a most powerful being, whom they call "God." At this point the little girl started running around the room in a burst of joy, saying, "I knew what you said wasn't true. It's Him! It's Him!" The grandmother was present during this. Though an atheist herself, she was the one who related this fact. When her father was speaking, the child felt he was betraying her in some way, but she could not defend herself because she was lacking the words. As soon as her father pronounced the word, she grasped it immediately and said, "It's Him! It's Him! I know what you were saying wasn't true."

This is only one of many experiences that led me to see that there is great religious potential in little children everywhere. In fact, it is so strong that I was forced to ask myself: Does there exist a mysterious bond uniting the young child with God?

JOURNEY WITH THE CHILD

The second approach to finding answers to these questions was to observe young children who are helped to draw near to God in some way. It is so important for us to observe children and their reactions, if we are to know what they receive with joy, and touches them deeply, or what remains only at the head level, because we want to hand on something that enriches their heart and their life as well as their mind. Certainly, it is necessary to know things, yet we should know with our heart, if I may use "heart" in its biblical sense, meaning our whole self.

It is important for us to know the aspect of God's love which corresponds to the needs of young children. To know what children really need may be the most urgent problem in religious education and catechesis today.

Essentially, the Christian message is to let people know that "God is love," as St. John says (1 John 4:7). However love can take so many forms. In the Bible, for instance, God is the bridegroom; there are many references to the spousal love God has for his people. Yet we cannot speak to a child about God as the bridegroom; this is the aspect of God's love that fulfills the longings of the adolescent or adult.

Of the infinite richness of love God offers us, what is the aspect of God's love that satisfies needs of young children? If we do not know what children truly need, there is a risk that what we say is on one level and what children hear is on another level. There is no meeting between the spoken words and the listening ears. It depends on our way of presenting God.

The image of Christ as the Good Shepherd is an example that helps to clarify this. When presenting the Good Shepherd parable to children, I noticed how eager the children were to hear it. They kept asking, "Tell me again. I want to hear it again." It was also striking to see that the children worked with the Good Shepherd materials over and over again (a wooden circular base for the sheepfold, and painted wooden figures for the shepherd and sheep). Many colleagues noticed this with children from very different countries. Then we started realizing the Good Shepherd touched a vital chord in the child's heart, that it satisfied some vital need.

Of course, the Good Shepherd is a Christological image that is fundamental in our Christian tradition, from the period of the catacombs up to the Easter Liturgy of today. The secret of the parable's resonance is that it corresponds to the young child's vital needs: the need to establish a relationship and the need for protective love. The young child is in a sensitive period for protection and the parable really satisfies the need for a protective quality of love.

---

[1] See Sofia Cavalletti, *The Religious Potential of the Child*, [Translated by Patricia M. Coulter and Julie M. Coulter] Liturgy Training Publications, Chicago, Illinois, 1992.

This is just one instance of the way children react when helped in their relationship with God. What is most significant is that the Good Shepherd (as well as the other themes mentioned later) evokes a similar response in children from different countries and environments. For example: Italy, from farming, working and middle-class families, and with gypsy children as well; Africa, with native children who are often without schooling of any sort; Mexico, from impoverished areas to upper middle-class areas; Argentina and Colombia; and in many communities in the United States and Canada.

There are many other examples in which it is not just the reaction of this or that individual child, but children in many places all responding in the same way. This reveals something of the actual potential of young children, gives us glimpses into their religious world, and prompts me to ask: Could this be *the* child?

THE RELIGIOUS WORLD OF YOUNG CHILDREN

When we are with children between the ages of three and six, we are really with persons in a different world. Children live in a different religious world. The way they live their relationship with God is quite different from ours. All of us know, for instance, that it is not possible to speak with a child of three about God as we would with an adult, and this can make things difficult for us. Let us pause awhile and step into their world, to catch some glimpse of their world.

One special feature of the religious life of children is the joy they are capable of when they are helped to draw near God. They feel a particular kind of joy.

Many things make children happy, but there are different qualities of happiness. There is a kind of happiness that makes children nervous, tense, and tired. The happiness that they feel when they come close to God is a quality of joy that makes them peaceful, relaxed, as if something very deep has been struck in their heart and they go on listening to this sound in the depths of their heart. It is like the response of someone who has found a life-giving place and, having found it, does not want to leave.

It is the kind of joy that involves children completely. After some children and I had prayed for a rather long time together, a little girl, Stefania, said, "My body is happy." It was as if she felt a physical joy in being with God. Children are totally involved in what they live. There is nothing left out when they pray or they hear the words of God.

There is always a response of this kind of joy when children listen to the Good Shepherd parable. They give the impression of being so comfortable with the Good Shepherd. The ease and spontaneity of young children's religious expressions and feelings spring from the depth of their hearts, as if it were completely natural to them.

These joyful responses are very significant since nothing is more gratifying than the satisfaction of a vital need. They tell us that religious formation is not something we impose. The religious experience is so deep and the serenity it gives is so great, that it responds to a vital need in the child. When we help the child to encounter God we are responding to the child's unspoken request: "Help me to come close to God. Help me to be fully who I am."

WHY RELIGIOUS EDUCATION SO EARLY?

Now we move to another level of questions that you may be asking or others have questioned you about:

- Is religious education necessary before the age of six?
- Why do you begin so early?
- Aren't three and four-year-olds too young?
- Isn't it better to wait until children are older? or in school? or when they have reached the "age of reason" (around six or seven)?

THE CHILD'S HUNGER

My response to these questions is based on the fact that the child is already a person, not just the future adolescent or adult-to-be. The child is a person with capacities and needs that cry out to be nourished now.

The first years of life are the most creative period. A number of psychologists say that 80% of all our capacities are formed by the age of three. If it is such a rich and creative period in every child's life, then it is an equally creative and important time for the child's religious growth and spiritual formation.

Young children not only have religious capacities but a particular religious *hunger* as well. When a child is hungry, he or she must be fed now, without waiting until tomorrow.

This hunger is not always easy for us to satisfy, because little children live their relationship with God in a very different way than we do. But this same fact is also the source of wonderful gifts that come to us when we do try to nourish their hunger for God. After all, God is not only the God of adults and, if Jesus said we are to be like little children to enter the kingdom of God, then they must have something to teach us.

THE YOUNG CHILD'S WAY

Let us spend some time speaking about these special religious needs and capacities that belong especially to early childhood, and the years before the age of six.

The young child's religious needs have already been mentioned. I prefer to speak to you with examples to show generally what I mean by the young child's religious *capacities*, and then I will highlight some of these specifically.

One day a group of women were visiting our catechetical center. They noticed a five-year-old girl who was mixing flour with yeast and without yeast to see the difference between the two batches of dough. (This is an activity relating to the parable of the leaven which will be addressed later in the book.) So I asked her if she could tell our visitors what she was doing, because it was rather unusual to see a child making bread! When I asked her she answered, "I am watching how the kingdom of heaven grows," as if she was really seeing the kingdom of God growing before her eyes.

Another example I recall happened at the beginning of my work in this field of early childhood religious education. I was presenting the sacrament of Baptism to a group of four to six-year-old children. I wanted to help them understand the meaning of the gesture of the imposition of the hands, the gesture of invocation of the Holy Spirit. I did not know what young children were capable of so I thought perhaps it was too difficult. Anyway I wanted to try. I took off my ring, put it in my hand, stretched out my hand and let the ring drop. I repeated this two or three times and then I said, "When I want to give you a gift, I must stretch out my arm and open my hand, otherwise the gift does not pass from me to you." Then I repeated the gesture once again without the ring saying, "When the priest does this gesture during baptism we do not see anything dropping from his hand, so why does he do that?" They answered almost as if I had asked an obvious question: "Because he gives us the Holy Spirit." It was so clear and simple to them.

THE CAPACITY TO ENJOY

Young children have a natural ability to enjoy their relationship with God in a very deep way. Children are very capable of enjoying the presence of God; they are able to give themselves totally to God's love. It is only before the age of six that children are completely inside this joy.

How important this is to realize. If we can enjoy the presence of God in our life, then our faith is established on the only sure foundation. Perhaps it is only when we enjoy God's love, only when we enjoy God's presence in our life, that we really have a vital faith, like Abraham's, something rooted very deeply in our life. If we are not allowed to enjoy God's presence, then there is always effort and struggle in our religious life; if there is only that it may mean that something is missing in our spiritual life.

The birth of the religious person occurs through the enjoyment of God's love. If children are helped to enjoy God, they really have a strong foundation for their religious life.

CAPACITY FOR PRAYER

Children have a tremendous capacity for prayer, which is why we will devote an entire chapter (Chapter 11) in this book to it. At this point I only want to mention how very beautiful their prayer is on the level of quality as well as quantity.

Young children's prayer is usually prayer of thanksgiving and praise. We can help their prayer correspond to and be an expression of their interior life if we guide them in this direction.

RADICAL SIMPLICITY

Young children are radical—meaning they go to the root of things—in their religious needs. They are satisfied only with the essentials, the core. Young children are free of the extras that often accumulate in our life.

Children can help us free ourselves from these inner complications and reach the level of simplicity they ask of us. I recall a little boy of three and a half who had been told about the Good Shepherd but he had not heard about guardian angels. When he first heard the words "guardian angel" he asked, "What is that?" It was explained to him that it is an angel that God gives us in order to protect and defend us. Then the child responded, "What do I need it for?" It was not a question of either/or, but the child was drawn to the more essential, the Good Shepherd.

This indicates the need to understand what children are really asking from us. Young children are our guides. When we are faithful to the essentials and try not to stray into areas of secondary importance, children follow us with enthusiasm and joy.

Children help us to become simple and essential. To live the religious experience with young children can be such an education for us.

CAPACITY FOR LOVE

Before six years of age the whole child is involved in what is being lived, including the relationship with God. With children after the age of six it is different; there is no longer this totality of being, they do not feel as free as they were before (see Chapter 7).

We know how much modern psychology stresses the importance of love in every aspect of human life. Love is the basis of our religious life as well. Young children really fall in love with God. It comes from the depth of their soul. Of course, it may happen for any of us at any moment of our lives, but before the age of six children fall in love quite naturally. If we start catechesis or religious education before the age of six, we begin building on the actual foundation floor and we are helping the child to establish a relationship of *being in love* with God.

Just as important, in beginning the child's religious formation before six years of age, we avoid two possible dangers: intellectualism and moralism.

The religious training many of us may have received was too intellectual and too moralistic. Many of us received information about God. It provided our mind with ideas but it did not warm our heart, in the sense of touching our whole person.

Besides the preoccupation with getting quick results in terms of behavior, this type of religious education did not allow us to encounter God free from worries about what we should or should not be doing. This may have hindered us from experiencing that quality of peaceful and serene enjoyment which the relationship with God cannot fail to give. Or, worse still, perhaps it distorted the face of God into that of a judge.

However, these defects—intellectualism and moralism—are almost inevitable when we begin the child's religious formation only after six years of age. You will see why when you look for a moment at some of the characteristics of the older child (after the age of six or seven):

- The child has new intellectual and cultural interests.
- The child's mind is opening to an objective and abstract form of thinking.
- The older child also begins to be interested in moral concerns.
- The child searches to know what "good" and "bad" means, and what "should" or "should not" be done.

Now here are the basic characteristics of young children we have been describing:

- Before the age of six, the child's whole person is involved.
- All the young child's faculties of mind and heart are engaged in an experience.
- The young child is able to surrender completely to what is being lived.

This is why early childhood is such a crucial period in the child's development. The young child's way of being totally involved, including all the capacities of intellect and emotion, is fundamental for his or her harmonious formation.

THE CHILD'S NEED FOR RELATIONSHIP

The child's deepest need is for relationship. We know that we grow and are formed through relationships. But we also know there are different degrees in which relationships contribute to our personal development and harmonious integration. I think it is possible to say that God is the necessary Partner the child needs for the fullest possible self-formation (we will say more about this later on in the second part of the book). When like finds like, enjoyment is born. The constant and repeated manifestations of joy children show in their relationship with God inclines me to say that the "image" of God, which is in all of us (Genesis 1:26), is reflected with a special transparency in children.

There is a special rapport between young children and God. Why is their relationship with God so spontaneous and joyful? Because in this covenant relationship with God, children find what is most precious in themselves: the capacity to love.

The relationship with God is basically an experience of love, of love without limits. In the covenant relationship there is a meeting between God who is "Love," and the child, who is so rich in love; different in their capacity and yet alike in their quality, they truly encounter one another. In the covenant relationship the child finds the Partner who is limitless, unfailing love, who meets the child's deepest need, and the child is in harmony with the world.

WHY CHRISTIANITY?

Before continuing, it is worthwhile to take a moment to address three questions that are asked frequently:

- Why introduce children to a specific religious tradition?

- Wouldn't it be better to cultivate a "religious sensitivity" in children? Couldn't this be used later to respond to a religious message?
- Isn't it better to help children be open to the beauty of nature, etc.?

In responding to these questions briefly I would like to offer these considerations:

- Wishing to stay on a vague level, without any specific content, is the same as wanting the child to talk but without using any particular language. If we want to speak of the religious reality, we need to use language.
- As for a specifically religious message, the Judaeo-Christian message is a basic part of our culture. Part of educating children means introducing them to their environment and the values it holds. This also helps the child to understand and appreciate other perspectives as well.
- As for choosing "the way of nature," the Christian message does inspire admiration for the beauty of nature, but it goes beyond this. The God of the Covenant creates a personal relationship with us here and now. The child cannot grasp this without hearing the Good News.

FOOD FOR THE CHILD'S HUNGER

Here are some of the biblical themes that provide the food necessary to nourish the child's hunger. It is important to say that we chose these themes not by our own planning but because they were the ones the children responded to most particularly. In following their lead, we discovered they guided us to the core of the Christian message, the fundamental themes that express the very essence of Reality.

What we offer to young children can be synthesized in two points:

- There is Someone who knows us and "calls us by name" (Christ the Good Shepherd).
- He gives us life (Christ the Light) and illumines us with the gift of his whole self, in unfailing love.

With this we center upon the mystery of Life itself, at its very origin.
We also center on the mystery of Life:

- The parables of the kingdom of God.
- These parables (mustard seed, precious pearl and so on) help us to meditate on that power that is within us and yet does not come from us, and on the force of Life in which we are immersed, which "grows" from a less to a more.

These are the pivotal points around which the entire Christian proclamation we give to children rotates. These satisfy the hunger of young children; they take hold of them with serenity and joy, and become meditative and still. The children's responses to these themes reveal how capable they are of going to the heart of the matter, and how this alone satisfies them.

The children's responses also indicate that we are not imposing on them by letting them draw near to the Christian message. Instead, the Christian proclamation gives us the means of introducing little children to Reality at its deepest level.

The second part of this book will develop the aspect of the Christian message in detail, specifically:

- The biblical themes which are our basis for the religious formation of children.
- How these are lived in a particular way in the Catholic tradition.
- The way these scriptural themes are lived in the liturgy, especially in Baptism and the Eucharist.

SERVANT OF THE COVENANT RELATIONSHIP

In closing, I would like to say that while there are many things to be done with older children, there is one thing to be done before the age of six: to help children fall in love.

We are helping a vital process and not just an intellectual process. Where life is concerned we feel powerless at times; we cannot go straight to the center. We cannot fall in love in the place of another person, but we can help that person meet Someone with whom to be in love.

Christianity is above all an event. Children cannot know that Christ died and is risen if they are not told and they need to know this. We need to speak to our children about God, to make the announcement, the proclamation.

How can we give this proclamation to children? This is what the second part of the book is about. For now it is enough to say that each of us can tell little children there is Someone who knows them and calls them by name, then it is the children themselves who fall in love. We have helped the relationship between the child and God be established, and we share in their joy as the servants of this relationship.

2. HELPING THE CHILD

Silvana Quattrocchi Montanaro, M.D.

Each child is an important person to you as parents and to God. These reflections and suggestions about the beginning of the young child's growth are offered to help you nurture your child's development in body, mind, and spirit.[1]

THE JOURNEY BEGINS: EDUCATION FOR LIFE

Let us begin by reflecting on the child's life before birth. How much has taken place during the nine months of pregnancy! The child grew from a very small living being who at the beginning could not even be seen. As new parts of the body develop and enlarge, not only is there physical growth taking place but also the child's mind is growing as well. On a practical level, the more you understand what is happening in your child's mind, the more you can appreciate and help your child's development.

EVERYTHING WE DO WITH CHILDREN IS EDUCATION

In order to help your child through the first phases of development, you need to know a few but essential things. The first of these is the fact that everything you do with your child is education.

Every encounter with your child is an educational moment, an occasion to bring forth some precious talent. Actually, a major part of the education or ideas conveyed to very small children

---

[1] [Editor's note: Dr. Montanaro's contribution was necessary in order to complete this book's treatment of the young child, by focusing on the earliest period of life—from before birth through the first three years. However, for the purpose of brevity, this chapter was shortened considerably, with the author's approval. Readers who wish a full and detailed discussion of this period are recommended to read Dr. Montanaro's book *Understanding the Human Being: The Importance of the First Three Years of Life* (Nienhuis Montessori USA, 1991) available from Nienhuis Montessori, 320 Pioneer Way, Mountain View, California 94041-1576.

This chapter is written from the perspective of the child's whole life-journey. In doing so, the author uses the word "child" when referring to all the various stages in the child's development, both pre- and post-natal. I have followed the author's usage, which is consistent throughout the chapter. P.C.]

happens through the every day tasks parents perform in caring for them; feeding and washing your child and going for a walk in the sunshine are just a few examples. It is precisely through these ordinary, daily activities that you contribute to your child's inner development, although this inner growth may not be as measurable as the child's physical growth. Every parent is an educator in the sense that you are helping children to develop their rich potential and setting the foundation for future development as well.

Pause a moment and reflect on the fact that in this process you are helped to develop your own inner richness, the "talents" the Gospel parable speaks about. Each child has a great mission: to grow and become a fully realized human being. This mission of becoming fully human persons is true for each one of us and lasts throughout our life. In the course of caring for children and establishing the foundation for their physical, intellectual, emotional and spiritual lives, we too are offered an opportunity for developing our own potential. When we are with children, if we realize we have a model for ourselves, as Christ said, we will discover that our relationship not only helps them but it helps us too.

PRENATAL LIFE

During the first part of life in the womb, the child has passed through many steps of development and is growing rapidly. This is achieved in a hidden manner, even before we realize that a living human being is present!

Let us recall together some of these significant steps, with a view to highlighting a few of the attitudes and responses they might suggest.

Of all the parts of the human body, the brain is the one which grows fastest. The brain and nervous system develop quickly during pregnancy because they provide the tools for understanding ourselves and the outside world, and for relating to the world around us from the very beginning of life. The brain provides a crucial capacity: the ability to remember. The memory stores experiences; and the brain becomes a storehouse of information and experiences that grows gradually each day. In light of this, you are invited to reflect on the following suggestions.

- Be attentive to the presence of this living human being—small in body but great in mental activity—who is growing so quickly during pregnancy.

- Mother and father, and every person in contact with an expectant mother as well, should be aware of and try to feel the presence of this new human being.

- To be a mother or father is to participate in God's own plan. Your help is needed to actualize your child's potentialities, and this begins from the time in the womb.

From the second or third month of pregnancy, the hearing mechanism is working and the brain begins storing the memory of voices.

- Convey to the child what is happening in the environment. For example, communicate with your child, not just in the sense of thinking about but actually talk to, address words to this living human being growing within you.

- Develop some kind of phrases, greetings, or songs to sing to your child. After birth, your child will remember this, which means that it will be possible for the child to recognize the parents' voices, the songs and whatever else they shared together before birth. I say parents because the father's voice, one of the most present in the environment, also reaches the child within the womb. In becoming aware of this from the very beginning, you can start your "service to life," as I call it, because helping the child is truly serving life.

During pregnancy, the child is not only capable of listening and hearing well, but also of participating in the mother's emotional life. If the mother is feeling happy or unhappy, the child is able to sense these feelings, because this is a participating (not a passive) person, a human being full of life and understanding, with a very great mind that is at work from the beginning of life.

- Praise God and give thanks together for the miracle that is being fulfilled during this first stage in the life of your child—a unique human being. Cultivate the awareness that, as your baby's life unfolds, a particular design of the Creator is taking flesh.

Recent research shows that from the seventh month of pregnancy, the child moves his or her mouth exactly at the same time as the mother is speaking. That is, the child reproduces the sounds the mother is making, and at the same time that the mother is speaking. It is important to realize, then, that just as the fetus is able to hear voices in the womb, to listen to music with you, and so forth, by the seventh month your child is also talking with you, as you are talking.

- Take time to become aware of the wonderful fact that not only does your child speak when you are speaking, but also that when you pray, your child prays too; when you are praying, your child is praying *with* you.

MOMENT OF PASSAGE: BIRTH AND THE FOLLOWING WEEKS

Birth is an important passage for mother and child; labor is a work you do together, and has a deep meaning for both of you. The time arrives when the child has reached a certain stage of development and must leave the womb to enter a wider world in which to continue to grow. For the mother's part, this is the time when you are sending forth your child in more than just the physical sense of giving birth. It is the time when, so to speak, you are saying to your child: "Now it is time for you to see more, to experience more, to enjoy a different type of life. I am helping you to go forth." This attitude can help your child's awareness of birth not as separation but as a new beginning. Even though a certain period is ending, your relationship is not ending. It now enters a new phase in family relationships.

After birth comes a special time in caring for your child. It is a time for a different quality of bonding between you and your child. The experience of the first weeks of life should lead your newborn to a feeling of personal security. The bond of love thrives on the joy of being together.

- Your manner of holding your child is a way to identify yourself with your child's needs and communicate this involvement.

- Your actions of handling your child, such as bathing and changing your baby, contribute to your baby's sense of reassurance and the feeling of well-being and joy that comes from being with you.

- Look at your child's daily needs as moments when you are offering your child an opportunity to be with you. Approach the everyday tasks you do with your child as very special moments of encounter between you and your child.

- See the daily repetition of what you do with your baby as occasions for offering your personal presence and experience to the child, as if you were saying: "Now I can be with you. I can know you better and you can know me better, so that we deepen our relationship."

Immediately after birth, there is a special time (about six to eight weeks) in which the mother's presence is crucial to a harmonious transition period for the infant between pregnancy and life outside the womb. It is a time when mother and child need to be protected so that when they are together it can be truly a time of mutual intimacy. The moment of feeding, for example, needs the mother's presence. Whether breastfed or bottlefed, your baby is receiving more than just nourishment. Your baby is receiving the presence of a very special person, the person known during pregnancy. Feeding is a moment of encounter. Ideally it should be the mother (or the person who is becoming the mother) who is present with the baby during feeding time.

During these weeks, everyday tasks on behalf of your child can be moments of close communion and mutual understanding. However this does not mean giving an inordinate amount of attention. It simply means responding to the child's needs. For example:

- Try to respond immediately when your child cries to see if something is needed. Perhaps there is too much air in the stomach and all that is required is simply to pick up your baby until it goes away. Or it could be enough just to place your baby in a position so as to be able to look around and see what is going on.

Other simple ways of responding come to mind when you recall that your baby needs adequate sensorial stimulation after birth. For instance, consider the following:

- Attach a mobile with colored objects to the wall.

- Put your child in an interesting place where there is something stimulating to look at or where the baby can see you moving around. This helps your child to see that you can continue your relationship together and that it is not necessary to be physically attached constantly.

- When feeding and caring for your child, look at and talk directly to your child. This contact and quality of presence create a deep personal relationship.

- At other times it is sufficient simply for the child to be able to see and hear you, or to look at the people around, or to see out a window to watch life outside change according to the season.

When your newborn receives this quality of attention in the first six to eight weeks, he or she not only receives a sense of personal security but also a basic trust in the world.

From a human point of view, all that you do during these first weeks and the following months can help your child to develop an attitude of confidence towards life, even when things become difficult. This is true not only from the psychological perspective but also from the religious point of view. We can be confident when we believe God's presence is always with us. God's life is in each of us. God's desire is to be in relationship with each of us and to help us to journey along the path of life.

THE FATHER'S PRESENCE

I would like to include a note to fathers. The emphasis on maternal care during this transitional period could lead to a mistaken impression that the father's presence is less important in the newborn's life. In actual fact, the father's presence is necessary from the very beginning of the child's life.

A father's presence is as necessary now as it was to start this new life. As parents you began the child's life together, and as the father you continue to be important in every moment of your child's life.

Here are a few basic suggestions for fathers to consider:

- Support your wife during pregnancy and share together the joy of this new life coming into the world. If you have been prepared, you could help your wife directly or indirectly during childbirth. When mother and baby come home, your presence is extremely important.

- It would be wise if you could plan some vacation time for the time when your wife comes home with your newborn, so that you are there as well to share the beginning of this new life. Your presence is necessary to offer a protective barrier between your wife and child from outside disturbances, so that the times when they need to be together (such as feeding time) can become moments of communion. The idea of paternity leave is not some strange dream! Countries such as England, Sweden, Norway and others have recognized the need for paternity leaves.

- You are as important in your child's life as the mother. Try to be present to do something special with your baby every day, (for example, bathing your child when you come home from work). During these moments, your child can create a special relationship with you and you can become father in the sense of bonding yourself to your child, and helping your child know you. This will help the whole family to share together in the joy the new child brings.

COMMUNICATING WITH YOUR CHILD

It is essential to communicate with your child. Every daily action done *to* your child and *with* your child is an opportunity for communication. From the very beginning, your child desires, more than anything else, a relationship of love and communication with you. Your child is a living person who is on a continual journey of creative self-formation. This process is always based on communication with you and the environment. Long before your child acquires verbal language, there are many opportunities to experience the joy of communicating with others.

Here are a few practical guidelines:

- Although newborns are little, they are able to communicate with us, but they have a different ways of communicating. They are very attentive in looking at you; they smile and laugh; they also try to move their body towards you, which is their way of communicating that they want to come and be close to you.

- Since the movements of small children are still very uncoordinated, try to be patient and not expect a quick response. You will see that when you try to communicate, your child will show great pleasure and will respond to you.

- Remember that your child's mind is very active and receptive. Your child is constantly absorbing many things, naturally and without effort; this is the special quality known as the *absorbent mind*. Since your child's brain is working constantly and storing information, the help you offer in the beginning of your child's life is important because it will become the material with which your child works later in life.

- Try to speak with your child in a certain way; be gentle and respectful. Cultivate a caring relationship with your child and among yourselves. All this will be absorbed, which means your child will learn to relate to others in the same respectful, gentle, and caring way.

THE CHILD'S WAY OF LEARNING

The brain's task is to receive information coming from within us and the world around us, to work with it, and then give responses. It bears the characteristics of our "image and likeness" to God. What you offer your child in these early years is especially important because learning happens in a different way at this time.

Another aspect to understand is that the wisdom of creation accompanies God's littlest children and gives them special abilities, but these are present only for a certain length of time. The developmental process is guided by inner sensitivities that direct your child toward specific activities, which in turn allow your child to acquire the abilities necessary to advance further. These special moments are called "sensitive periods."[2]

In the first years from birth onwards, there are three sensitive periods: order, movement, and language. I will explain these briefly and give a few practical ideas for helping your child with regard to these special needs.

---

[2] [Editor's note: What follows is the author's brief synthesis on the special areas of the child's growth and development. For an in-depth treatment, the reader is referred to Dr. Maria Montessori's book *The Secret of Childhood*, Barbara Barclay Carter, ed. (Orient Longman, Bombay, 1986) P.C.]

THE NEED FOR ORDER

There is a need for order, especially from the beginning of the child's life through the first two years. The child needs an environment in which things are, as far as possible, in their own place. The sense of order also prepares the child to understand about the dimensions of space and time. Without going into many psychological details, it is important to do things with small children according to a routine which respects these aspects of space and time. Briefly, try to have order in what you do with children, and where and when you do it with them.

A way to help your child's need for order is to do certain activities at the same time and place:

- Choose one particular place where your child is changed. If you use one particular place then your child has that particular view of the environment, starts to understand what is going on, and knows that you will talk with him or her, and so on. This makes life very reassuring and secure for your baby. Routine gives small children a sense of security because it allows them the time to understand things and this is why our attentiveness to place is so important.

Feeding is another example:

- Choose one place where you always nurse or feed your child, such as a comfortable chair in a certain corner. When your child is there in your arms and looks around, it becomes a familiar place. Then your child can see the constant relationship among the various objects and persons he or she lives with and will be able to build up a sense of order which becomes internal. This means that the child will become a person capable of establishing order around him or her because it has been built and internalized at the right time.

THE NEED FOR MOVEMENT

Another important sensitive period is for movement. Even inside the womb—where there is certainly very little space—the child is moving and using all the parts of his or her body. After birth your child needs opportunities to develop some kind of voluntary movement, the type of movement that enables your child to actualize a thought or idea. The little child needs your help in order to express movement freely. The way you dress your child and the places you put your child are two examples of helping the development of movement.

Two other points of interest are:

- Free movement does not mean that your baby can go everywhere or that everything is to be put at your child's disposal. It means simply that from birth onwards, your child has a space in which to move freely (such as a low bed or blanket on the floor).
- When you help your child's expression of movement, especially in the first and second year of life, it builds a sense of self-confidence and your child will be able to make the effort to respond when the challenges are bigger.

THE NEED FOR LANGUAGE

The third sensitive period is for language. Children learn a language in a short time—in the first two years of life—yet even at the end of the first year they understand almost everything you tell them. The child achieves this with the aid of the absorbent mind. The child listens to people, the sounds and words are stored in a special part of the brain, and the child comes to understand that each sound and word corresponds to an object. From the very beginning, the child starts storing the sounds and words of language that will be used later in an ever more perfect way. Consider these simple ways to help your child's language:

- During the time of pregnancy, it is helpful to talk to the baby.
- After birth, when talking to your baby, speak slowly and clearly (careful not to overwhelm with words).
- Show your child the object you are using and/or the activity you are doing, naming it, and repeat this routine often.

These are basic ways to enrich vocabulary and language from the beginning, giving your child an additional richness he or she can use all through life.

A BIG STEP TOWARDS INDEPENDENCE: WEANING

Around five or six months of age your child has finished the reserve of iron stored while in the womb. Now the baby has special enzymes from the digestive system and in the saliva which enable the digestion of food. During this time, the child starts teething. Also around this age, the baby is becoming able to sit up and shows a great interest in the environment. This is the time to introduce the child to new types of food. The food is new in that: 1) it is other than milk, such as vegetables, fruits, and eggs; 2) it is eaten in a different way, now that the baby is able to chew.

Some simple pointers to help this process are:

- Give the food with a spoon so that your child can chew and taste it. When you change your child's food, also change your child's way of eating it.
- Sit your child in front of you when you give these new foods so that you can look at each other face to face. This helps your child understand that the relationship with you is changing. Being able to sit up at a table, the baby manifests a different "I" or "me." It is also the start of that quality of face-to-face relationship with others that will continue for your child's whole life.
- Eating solid foods provides an opportunity for more active participation on your child's part. Gradually help your child to eat by himself or herself (and at his or her own rhythm). For instance, cut the food into small pieces so that your child can take it with hands or spoon. This helps your child to be more independent and to realize: "I can do it by myself."
- Help your child to drink from a little glass. Trust, you will see that your baby is able and can do it well.

Children enjoy this new way because they see that this is how you eat and drink, and like to be able to eat the way you do.

"HELP ME TO DO IT BY MYSELF"

Helping little children in their own efforts to grow is truly a form of service. The child's intense desire is, "Help me to do it by myself." You can respond to this request on your child's part simply by:

- Doing only what is necessary, because your child is growing quickly and is capable of doing a little more each day.
- Showing your child how to do things and then facilitating your child's own personal efforts.

Consider for a moment the way God invites our collaboration. In relation to God we are more dependent than the child is in relation to us, yet God puts us in the heart of creation, gives us the whole world and says, "This is all for you. Do what you can. Use it responsibly and wisely." God invites us to be co-workers in creation. Recall this in your relationship with your child and your attitude becomes the attitude of someone who receives an important person—as your child really is—who has great potential needing your help to grow. You become collaborators with God in the creation of the human person precisely by helping your child to develop this inner richness. For instance, you are doing this when:

- You not only do things for your child but help your child to do things with you as well.

- You invite your child's collaboration until you see that your child is able to do things unaided.

- You step aside so as to give more space for your child's own activity (because this is the goal you are encouraging your child to reach).

FURTHER DEVELOPMENT OF MOVEMENT

Movement provides the child with the means for interacting with the environment and the persons in it. Coordinated movement is psychologically important because it enables the child to gain independence, self-esteem, and the chance to take an active part in life. For a child, independence means: "I can do what I need to do and I can reach the persons and things I want without always having to depend on others." To be independent is a valuable experience for the child. It is as if the child were to say: "I am able to resolve my own problems" (which produces feelings of self-worth) "and this gives me a sense of security" (which is a basic trust in oneself).

Therefore, try to help your child use the new abilities he or she is developing. Help any new movements your child is capable of and any new expression of independence he or she manifests. This can happen in simple ways, for instance:

- During bath time, provide a small sponge or cloth and invite your child to wash himself or herself. In this way you are establishing a spirit of working with your child and your child becomes an active participant.

This quality of collaboration is possible even with small children. For example:

- When you are dressing your child, say: "Give me your hand," or "Put your foot here," and your child will understand you much sooner than you might think.

- Encourage whatever your child is able to do and you will nurture his or her self-confidence and joy in life.

Not only does your child's own development increase in this way, but your child's relationship with you becomes more collaborative.

THE GROWING CHILD: 3–6 YEARS OF AGE

From three to six years of age is a period when your child perfects the abilities already gained and expands the knowledge and experience acquired of the world, others, and oneself. Let us reflect briefly on three characteristics of this period and a few concrete considerations they imply.

First, your child's desire to do things with you continues to be characteristic of the years from three to six. From a practical standpoint, this suggests that you:

- Help your growing child to participate in the activities involved in personal and family life: washing, dressing, preparing food, setting the table, and all the activities your child is able to do.

- Provide opportunities for broader cultural activities; offer your child simple explanations for these and encourage your child's active participation in them.

- Try to be patient and slow down your pace when you are with your child. Helping your child to develop—the purpose of education—is not something that can be achieved quickly.

The second characteristic is the beginning of a sensitive period for culture. Your child is ready for wider cultural experiences, beyond the context of family and home environment, and could begin school. Whether in school or not, your help is needed so that your child can enrich his or her great potentialities and be able to develop them. Two fundamental ways of doing this are: to continue to invite your child to collaborate in family activities; and to give more and more space to your child's own activity.

A third feature of this period is that it marks the beginning of a new search in your child's life: your child seeks to know the reasons for everything. Here are a few of the practical implications you may want to consider:

- Respond to your child's desire to know and in a clear but essential way.

- Be prepared to answer difficult questions (the concern about death may arise) and try to find the most suitable way of doing so.

- Be willing to meditate on the values you want to pass on to your child (in response to your child's right to the truth).

"BECOME LIKE A LITTLE CHILD"

We have been considering some of the basic ways of helping your child's human potential. Your presence is so valuable that the simple, everyday ways of being and doing with your child will bear great fruit in your child's life. The small ways you help your child during these formative years will contribute significantly to your child's growth. All that you offer helps your child to become a person who is capable of doing things, who feels part of the family and society, and who looks at life in a positive way. Your child will be a person who can praise God for the gift of life and develop this beautiful gift not only for his or her own personal growth but for the growth of humanity as well.

By reflecting on these developmental factors, we see the way the child invites us to look within ourselves so as to understand ourselves better and our world too. This is how the child draws us along a path of personal growth and offers us a precious opportunity to discover or recover our own hidden "talents" that the Gospel tells us about. And, I believe, this is the reason why Jesus placed the child before us as a model and opportunity for taking part in the kingdom of God.

3. PRACTICAL SUGGESTIONS

Gianna Gobbi

In this brief section I will offer a few practical suggestions that will be of some assistance to parents, as well as teachers and catechists concerned with the young child's religious development. Let us begin by considering the importance of the environment, because the environment is essential in order for life to begin and develop.

THE IMPORTANCE OF THE ENVIRONMENT

The word "environment" has many connotations. One way to understand it is to see it as everything that surrounds us: the earth and the universe. All living organisms, whether animal or vegetable, require a special biological environment, such as seas, mountains, deserts, etc. These natural environments offer life support systems that differ according to the needs of each living species; for example, a fish cannot live out of water. We, however, as humans, are capable of adapting to every biological environment.

We need another sort of environment to foster the social, moral, and cultural elements of our life as well. The first of these environments is the family—the primary environment—then school and other institutions. The environment that nourishes our religious life is the community of believers, the Church. Naturally, every environment differs in relation to the purpose for which it is intended and to the kind of activity that takes place there.

THE CHILD'S SUPPORT SYSTEM

Modern education strongly emphasizes the importance of the environment for the child's formation. Basically, the environment truly helps the child's development when it is prepared in a way that corresponds to the needs of the child.

Recall for a moment that first and foremost, the environment is composed of persons. You are the key component in your young child's support system. It also includes the furnishings and objects which you have chosen and arranged there. It is important to be aware that these objects are the indirect instruments or tools in your child's process of education.

In this light, we will address how to prepare the environment and these instruments in relation to the age of the child so as to serve the child's needs. These needs change according to the various developmental stages the child goes through. First, we offer a few suggestions about the environment parents can prepare in the family for young children up to six years of age, and then we will speak about the environment to be used specifically for religious education of young children.

THE CHILD IN THE FAMILY

GENERAL ENVIRONMENT

The essential elements to keep in mind in preparing an environment which helps the child's particular needs are: 1) movement, 2) language and 3) order, since the newborn has a special sensitivity for acquiring and developing these.

A few simple suggestions with respect to these three building blocks are:

- A bed or crib that is large enough so as not to hinder your child's vision of the environment.
- A colored mobile (in stylized forms such as birds, fish, etc.) beside the crib or bed which will attract your child's attention and stimulate your child's hand movement.

In choosing toys for your child, remember that not all respond to the real needs and interests of young children. Try to select those which are necessary or useful in helping your child to develop the capacity for hand movement. There is also much in your own home environment to offer. Look around your home for objects that are suitable to your child's age. For instance, when the child is a little bigger you can adapt:

- Little boxes for opening and closing.
- Small bottles with tops that can be screwed on and off.
- Small containers filled with pebbles or some other substance that will make loud and soft sounds when shaken.

In using such objects, the child develops the capacity for movement and the manual ability of grasping and holding. At the same time, they stimulate your child's auditory sense. A few suggestions that will help your child's development of movement and language are:

- Place your baby on a blanket on the floor in the same room where the adults are. The baby will have the maximum possibility of movement on the blanket. Soon you will see your baby pivoting on the stomach and going round in circles, trying to move around, crawl, and roll onto one side in attempts to gain mastery of his or her body. Your child is able to watch your activities and also become familiar with the sounds of the human language and learn how to reproduce them.
- When caring for your child, say the names of the things you are using and the actions you are doing, and repeat these using the correct pronunciation and try to speak the words clearly and slowly.
- You may even want to arrange a bed that is very low and without sides (mattress style) that allows your child to be free to get in and out of bed when ready to do so.

Two important reminders are:

- Remember how important it is to respect the order of things in your home environment, and that the activities you do in taking care of your baby, such as feeding or changing, always take place in the same location. This is important not only for practical or hygienic reasons but also because the baby needs to see objects always in their own place in order to be able to establish points of reference. This provides an orientation in space and it enables your baby to construct and internalize a sense of order.

- When the process of weaning begins, around five or six months, your child can be seated at a low table to eat and all foods other than milk can be given with a spoon (especially important now that your child has the ability to chew and savor the taste of food). These are simple ways of helping your child make steps on the path to independence.

At six to seven months of age, you can help your baby's progress in development of movement by:

- Placing a sturdy stool or low table in the environment; your baby can use this as support for standing up and walking around and without any assistance on your part. You may be surprised to discover how simple objects like a bed, table, or chair can offer an opportunity for increasing your child's motor ability, while allowing your child to be personally active in an independent way.

- During this period it also helps if you allow your baby to crawl freely around the house on all fours (try not to worry too much about the child getting dirty) and to go up and down stairs (with your watchful presence).

Another brief reminder:

- As your child grows, the home continues to offer many opportunities for your child's development and independence particularly when you invite your child to do things with you, such as to help prepare the food, set the table, and other everyday activities, adding bit by bit whatever will help your child's need to grow and to develop intellectually.

RELIGIOUS ENVIRONMENT

Each aspect of our lives requires an environment in which to live it. This is true for our religious life as well.

In the family context, some basic ways you can help, even before your baby can sit up or move on its own, are to:

- Put a sacred image close to the crib and point it out to your child, such as an image of the Risen Christ, or the Mother of God with the child Jesus. The most simple and artistic representations are best. (For example, the works of Giotto or Fra Angelico are suitable for their solemnity and beauty of design.)

- Invite your child to watch and hear you when you perform sacred gestures, such as the sign of the cross when blessing your food. Bless yourself with the sign of the cross slowly and in silence, at other times give thanks to God praying with words.

- Bless your child with the sign of the cross, after you have finished a moment in which you have been caring for your child's physical needs.

- Gather together for morning and evening moments of prayer beside the baby's crib. Sing in a soft voice while nursing or feeding the child.

When your child is a little older, you may consider preparing a corner of your child's bedroom as a place for prayer (if this is possible) or choose another space in the home. It could be furnished with:

- A child-sized table, chest, or shelf.

- A beautiful sacred image (three dimensional images that show the whole shape are preferable).

- A candle or two (in a protective holder, vigil light style if you prefer).

- A small rug or cushion to kneel or sit on.

In the evenings, you (or whoever is taking care of the child) may invite the other brothers and sisters to come together here for a quiet moment of recollection. This time together, praying a short prayer or singing a song, and perhaps repeating these a few times, will become a ritual your child will look forward to and love to do every night.

Another obvious suggestion is to introduce your child to the environment of your church. A few practical guidelines to keep in mind are:

- When you go for a visit, give your child enough time to observe the people and things in the environment.

- When able to walk, offer your child the opportunity to explore the surroundings with you.

- When you go to Mass or some celebration in the church, help your child to see the people and to follow the actions of the celebrant at close range.

A SPECIAL PLACE: SCHOOL AND PARISH ENVIRONMENTS

A special place can be set aside in the parish or school to be dedicated to the religious education of young children, a space specifically for their spiritual formation.

This space, like any other educational environment, should foster independence and the development of movement by encouraging and respecting the child's own activity. This room or space (such as a part of a classroom) has its own particular characteristics to offer: 1) it differs from the classroom in that it has a special atmosphere which helps children to listen to the Christian message and reflect on and experience these religious truths according to their own way and pace (which is different from adults); 2) this room or space differs from the church too, because not only is the Word of God proclaimed and celebrated here but it is also a place where children engage in activities of their own. This room or space is an environment where the child's activity unfolds in a meditative and prayerful manner.

Whether it is a room in the parish or school building or a space in a classroom, preparing this environment requires a choice of materials and an arrangement of furnishings that will facilitate and invite this special quality of activity. Think of it in terms of a spiritual retreat center which, with the assistance of certain external elements, helps the child's concentration and reflection. At a retreat center, we find a variety of aids to help us to become calm and recollected, such as books, tapes, and so forth. In this environment the child finds this same kind of help especially through the use of certain materials (see below).

If you are interested in preparing such a room (if available) or space, the following suggestions may prove helpful.

- The furnishings should respond to the young child's needs at this developmental stage (low in height, easy to move, etc.).

- The objects and furniture (tables, chairs, and so on) must be adapted in size and weight to the child's strength and abilities. In this way the child will be able to move about freely, sit down, stand up with ease, move and use the objects according to the purpose for which they are designed.

Some essential materials to consider including in this space or room for children are:

- The Bible: it should occupy a central place; choose a beautiful edition; display it in a place of honor.

- Scripture booklets: for children who can read, you could provide individual booklets, each of which contains a single event or episode. (For example, the events surrounding Christ's birth and resurrection, and the parables of the kingdom.) These booklets should contain the actual biblical wording, written in large, simple letters so that they can be easily read.

- Parable of the Good Shepherd: a special place can be set aside for the Scripture booklet and the materials relating to the Good Shepherd parable. (These materials consist of small, two-dimensional wooden figures representing the main characters and features of the parable: Good Shepherd, sheep, sheepfold.)

A particular feature of this place or room to consider is an area for prayer. This is possible to arrange even in the home or classroom setting. Some of the features and activities which could be included in the prayer area are:

- Special care is given to the part of the room dedicated to prayer, both on your part and the child's.

- Put a shelf, or prayer table in a suitable location (accessible to the child).

- The children can take care of this area themselves, decorating it in relation to the seasons of the liturgical life of the Church.

- Invite the child(ren) to put a colored cloth on the shelf or table, hang a colored drape, choose an image to place on the prayer table, and so on. The colored cloths, drape, and various images are changed according to the liturgical season the Church is celebrating (purple for Advent and Lent; white for the feasts of Christmas and Easter; green for "ordinary time" between specific seasons; red for Pentecost, the feast of the Holy Spirit).

- There can be flowers which the child(ren) can arrange and care for; candles; and a small kneeler or simple floor cushions which allow the child(ren) to remain in prayerful recollection.

- The beginning of each liturgical season is an opportunity for celebration with related songs and prayers, during which the child(ren) can be invited to change the colored cloths, images, and so forth. To create an atmosphere conducive to prayer you could, for instance, slightly dim the lights to highlight the candle light, especially during the celebration of the Liturgy of Light, part of the Easter Vigil liturgy.

If your space (or classroom) is large enough, or if you have a room in a parish or school building, other suggestions to consider are:

- One area of the room may be dedicated to the materials on Baptism, and another area for the materials relating to the Eucharist. These materials would include scaled-down models (such as a baptismal font and an altar) that are smaller than child-size. Also, the associated objects which are proportionately reduced in size could be included (for instance, the containers for the water and oils in the Baptism area, and the altar vessels and liturgical color exercises in the Eucharist area).

- Another area can be set aside for materials on the parables of the kingdom, such as the mustard seed, the leaven, and the precious pearl (see the curriculum section, *Appendix B* of the book).

- An area may be arranged for the materials relating to the events in the life of Christ. A set of shelves with boxes containing the figures and environments for the events of Christ's infancy (such as the visitation of Mary to Elizabeth, the birth of Jesus, etc., with the Scripture booklets to accompany each); the materials associated with the events surrounding the death and resurrection of Jesus, such as the figures of Christ and the apostles and the model for the upper room of the Last Supper.

- Another area may be allocated to geographical materials, such as various forms of the land of Israel maps, highlighting the places associated with the principal events in the life of Christ (Nazareth, the announcement of the Incarnation; Bethlehem, the birth place of Jesus; Jerusalem, the site of the resurrection).

Whether your environment is part of a classroom or home, or a room set aside in the parish or school, the religious experiences lived here are oriented in such a way as to be reflected in the child's everyday life. Above all, the children's experiences here are intended to prepare them to take an active part in the life of the Church, particularly when the community of faith gathers together for the Eucharist and other celebrations.

A WORD ABOUT THE MATERIALS

The catechetical materials we have been discussing are basically:

1)   Designed for the child's use rather than as teaching aids for the adult. The specific purpose of these materials is to help the child's meditation and prayer.

2)   Constructed to engage the children's sensory-motor abilities and invite their interest. They are composed of objects which concretize the themes from the Bible and liturgy (in wood, plaster, cloth, etc.) and assist the child to personalize them.

PRESENTING THE MATERIALS TO CHILDREN

The following are some general guidelines in relation to the catechetical materials and how to help your child(ren) use them:

- The biblical or liturgical theme is presented. After reflecting on this theme with the child(ren), the materials relative to this theme are presented and the children are shown how they are used.

- Afterwards the materials are made available in their own place in the room for the children to use when and as often as they want. The children are given the opportunity to use the materials without your direct assistance. This is the time for the child to interiorize the Word of God you have proclaimed.

- After the children have been shown how to use the materials (and where they are kept), they are given freedom to choose what they wish to work with (because the materials respond to the child's needs at this stage of development).

- The child may repeat an activity as many times as it is necessary for him or her to do so. In the course of this repetition, the child may show great concentration while doing an activity. This is the fruit of the interaction between the child's own activity and the peaceful atmosphere in the room.

- Welcome the fact that a child may draw apart to work with a material alone and could continue to do so for quite awhile. This is a moment for absorbing and internalizing the theme (of the Christian message) that has been presented.

It is important to mention that this approach is flexible in presenting the materials to children. The sequence is adaptable; it is intended to serve both the Word of God and the child. It may be helpful to clarify this sequence with a summary, in step form. The presentation of a parable material will be used as an example:

- Begin by narrating the content of the parable in your own words (staying as close to the biblical text as possible).

- Guide the child(ren) towards an awareness that there is a deeper meaning to be discovered in the parable (this is the time for listening and reflecting together with the children).

- Read the parable (biblical text) solemnly.

- Present the materials to the child(ren).

- Move the materials (objects and/or figures) according to the sequence of action described in the parable (the biblical text).

- Return the material to the place where it is kept.

- Invite the children to use the materials, on their own if they wish.

GOOD NEWS FOR THE CHILD AND US

How beautiful upon the mountains are the feet of the messenger who announces peace, who brings good news.—Isaiah 52:7

This brief section has centered on two wonderful ways of helping the child's religious development, whether you companion the child's religious journey as a parent, teacher or catechist:

- Your part in religious education is necessary especially when you offer the proclamation of God's Word.
- Your preparation of the environment and the materials is also a very important service to the child.

In this process it will be necessary at times to step aside so as to support the child in an indirect way, and to allow the Word of God to carry out its work in a personal dialogue between child and Master. Also, it will require a certain delicacy to be attentive and ready to offer help when the child needs it, and to respond in a way that calls forth the child's own response.

In this we have every reason to be confident, because the environment and the materials help *us* as well. They provide us with a means of serving the child, while enabling us to maintain an attitude of reverence. They help us to respect the child's dignity, while encouraging the child's own activity. Above all, we can go forward on our journey with great confidence because the "power at work within us is able to accomplish abundantly far more than all we can ask or imagine" (Ephesians 3:20).

PART TWO

Sofia Cavalletti
Patricia Coulter

4. SOURCES OF NOURISHMENT

This part of the book will address in detail the Christian message as well as some of the practicalities involved in its communication to children. To begin, it is helpful for us to clarify a few principles and challenges underlying the concrete aspects—the *what* and *how*. This gives us a basis on which to build together.

SPEAKING ABOUT GOD WITH CHILDREN

First, we know we can never speak adequately about God. When it comes to children we may feel even more powerless. Sometimes, we may want to avoid the subject of religion altogether, for fear of making mistakes with children. However, this is not really a solution since silence itself can be a mistake.

QUESTION OF CONTENT: WHAT TO SAY?

The Catholic tradition offers us a rich deposit from which to draw. In regard to content we have a wealth of sources at our disposal: the Bible, the liturgy, and the magisterium of the Church. If we hold faithfully to these, we will have a secure foundation.

CHOICE OF METHOD: HOW TO SAY IT?

Second, there is the question of method. How do we speak about God with children?
The question of choosing a suitable method is an important concern in that it can help or hinder us and the children. If our choice of method corresponds to the nature of the content we are trying to communicate, we have a vehicle that is compatible with the message; if it does not, there is a danger of distorting it.

CALL TO INTIMACY

There are two concerns to consider in relation to method. The first of these requires a brief point of historical background.

In the last thousand years, much of theological thinking tended toward the abstract and intellectual. As a result, catechesis often abandoned the eloquent language of images in favor of theological definitions or explanations. Frequently this approach meant the message was defined or explained and presented to children from a propositional perspective alone. Therefore, it is primarily a form of religious training that imparts abstract information.

This is why it is crucial to find a method that is compatible with the religious message, one that conveys rather than limits the content, especially as the content we are referring to is the Mystery of the infinite God, revealed as an inexhaustible source of richness for us. The final words of St. John's Gospel indicate:

> But there are also many other things that Jesus did: if every one of them were written down, I suppose that the world itself could not contain the books that would be written (John 21:25).

The second concern to be addressed is finding a method that helps the young child to encounter this Person. If catechesis is to put the child "not only in touch but in communion, in intimacy, with Jesus Christ" (*On Catechesis in Our Time*, No. 5), what method helps us to do this in a way that avoids putting ourselves and our experience between God and the child?

We are invited to apply to ourselves "the mysterious words of Jesus: 'My teaching is not mine, but His who sent me'" (*On Catechesis in Our Time*, No. 6). What great respect is needed in the presence of God's Word, which even Jesus himself says is not his. Therefore, we need a method to ensure the objectivity asked of us, and to avoid the risk of clouding God's Word with our own words.

THE POWER OF SIGNS

Scripture and the tradition of the Church provide us with a way to respond to this call to communion: the method of signs. What is the meaning of signs in this context?

THE MEANING OF SIGNS

The sign is made up of a visible and tangible element which points to and contains a reality beyond our senses. St. Augustine said of the sign, "You see one thing, you understand another." We see light, bread, and wine, and through these we gradually come to the gift of God, the presence of God, and make it our own.

The sign refers to a reality that is different from what our senses perceive; it relates to a reality beyond our senses. The sign does not limit our perception. Rather, the sign always leaves the door open for further investigation.

Although the sign stays rooted in the visible and the tangible, it does not become imprisoned in it. This quality makes the sign especially compatible with the proclamation of the Message. While neither limiting nor exhausting the content of the message, the sign invites children to receive the message and respects their developing ability to penetrate the meaning of the Mystery involved.

SIGNS AS A SOURCE OF WONDER

Although poor in itself, the sign offers us a source and avenue into the richness of the Christian mystery that is inexhaustible. In this light, the nature of the sign can be said to be a poverty containing great richness.

The person who beholds a sign realizes that whatever level of understanding has been attained there is another level and yet another, and so it continues without ever reaching its depth. The person who contemplates the sign sees reality with a sense of wonder that is always growing.

Wonder is an essential dynamic of the human spirit and of our religious life as well. It is the basis of all understanding; even in ancient times Plato said, "Philosophy has no other origin but wonder." Wonder brings us the awareness that we can never fully fathom the reality we are living.

THE CHILD'S CAPACITY FOR WONDER

This quality of wonder is a special characteristic of young children. Wonder is a treasure needing to be cultivated in the spirit of the little child.

Wonder is also like a flower that requires, so to speak, a specific climate so that it will flourish and not wither. This climate is the opportunity to be able to stop awhile and dwell on reality, since wonder is not for those who are superficial or in a hurry. It is the offspring of the contemplative spirit in us.

Children have an immense capacity to pause and ponder, to contemplate the meaning of things. When we are proclaiming the Christian message it is helpful to give children the opportunity to reflect and meditate on it. By centering the children's attention on one theme, we give them the chance to stop and be still; if we change the object of their attention too often or too quickly, they set up a sort of defense against this, usually in the form of indifference. If we do not give children time to slow down and reflect restfully, then everything will end up seeming the same to them and they will lose interest.

So, when we introduce children to the religious reality through signs, we need to take our time and to give children time too. Children must be allowed enough time to gaze upon signs in their deepest dimensions, because signs disclose their endless wealth to them and to us in a gradual, unfolding way.

The whole world, and everyone and everything in it is a sign of God, telling us about God and helping us to know God.[1] As well as these basic signs, there are others that have taken on a fundamental importance in our Christian tradition: water, bread and wine, to name only the greatest. There is a specific bond between these signs and Christianity. What a wonderful contribution it is to children's religious formation when we introduce them to these signs in Scripture and in liturgy and help them read the rich meaning in these signs. The parables are one of the best ways for us to do this.

PARABLES

Among the biblical signs, a particular place belongs to the parable, *the teaching method* of Jesus (Mark 4:34).

The parable, like every sign, relates to a reality that is different from the episode or event it contains. For instance, the parable may speak of a woman making bread, but its aim is to introduce us to the kingdom of God.

Parables usually have two components: one is taken from everyday life, and the other from the transcendent level of reality. These two levels are like the two rails in a track that guide our meditation, helping us to go farther and deeper. The episode or event of the parable is like the façade of a house, behind which are several rooms filled with many treasures; to enter we need to go slowly, almost as if on tip-toe, and with a spirit of reverence.

---

[1] (See Chapter 7 on the Parables of the Kingdom.)

OFFERING A TREASURE

This is the kind of spirit we mean: to offer children the parables as we would a treasure so that it implants itself deep inside them and they can draw on it, how and when we do not know (Mark 4:27). Here are a few general indications for helping this to happen.

- Tell the parable's content in your own words to the children and then help them to enter into its meaning.

- This can be done especially by listening to God's Word together with children and engaging their innate capacity for wonder.

- Offer children points for reflection (in the form of wondering together rather than statements) to evoke their own response to the parable. Their response will be seen often in a calm and meditative attitude. This attitude is glimpsed more through the children's facial and body expressions than in their words.

- These reflections are gentle promptings for personal meditation both on the children's part and *ours*. For example, with the parable of the Good Shepherd, spend time reflecting with the children on: "How much the Good Shepherd cares for his sheep...He knows them...calls them by name....Who do you think the sheep are?"

- When reflecting together in this way, do not expect a quick response from the children. If a response is to be personal and deep, then it needs time to come forth. The emphasis is on helping children realize there is an infinity of things to discover in parables and that it is only when we live with parables that we enter gradually into their great scope.

Experience shows that when the parable is presented in this way it continues to act like yeast in the child's spirit and encourages the child to go more fully into its meaning.

GIFTS FOR US

When speaking about God with children it is valuable to keep in mind that the message we are announcing is addressed not only to the children but to us as well.

It is necessary for the child who is coming to know and experience new things to hear God's Word proclaimed, yet it is just as necessary for us. We need the opportunity to probe more deeply into things that often remain on the surface of life, so that our experience of encounter stays vibrant and the message retains its living and active quality within us (Hebrews 4:12).

To proclaim God's Word, however, does not mean assuming the role of an expert but simply serving God and children in a particular way. To serve in this way does not change what should be our habitual stance before God's Word: an attitude of openness, in a spirit of joy, wonder and gratitude, to the presence of a gift that reveals itself to us as ever greater.

It can be so inspiring for us to place ourselves in the position of listening to God's Word *with* children. Typically, children easily involve us in that wondrous admiration and help us to regain certain aspects of the Christian message, to keep vital wellsprings flowing in us. Thanks to children, the sense that the relationship with God is joy—above all else—will remain especially alive in us. This will enable us to free ourselves from somber aspects that perhaps still linger from a certain type of religious formation.

Listening to Scripture with others is always an enriching experience. This is especially true when listening together with children since God's Word resonates in a different way in children than in adults. Through children another echo of God's Word reaches us. This happens on the condition that we remain open to listening, and remember to speak only in the measure we are listening.

5. JESUS, THE GOOD SHEPHERD

Since Christ is the fullest manifestation of God, we center on the person of Jesus when speaking about God's love to children. We focus especially on Jesus as the Good Shepherd using two parables in particular.

BEING CALLED BY NAME

The first is the parable of the Good Shepherd, found in the tenth chapter of St. John's Gospel. The theme of the shepherd who calls and the sheep who are listening to his voice, introduces the child to the reality of the covenant relationship. The covenant theme is central to the Bible: God in search of us and our response to God's initiative.

The element of the parable that strikes young children is the fact that the shepherd knows and calls each sheep by name. This reveals in an explicit way that the Good Shepherd has a personal relationship with each one of us.

At the same time this parable also creates in children an openness to others. The relationship with the Good Shepherd is both personal and communal, because it develops from the "womb" to the "flock." This is often highlighted in children's drawings which show the shepherd calling different names and in others where the sheep are each identified by name. Laura, five years old, wrote: "I love the shepherd and I love the sheep."

"JUST FOR ME"

The second parable is the "found sheep" in the Gospel of St. Luke, chapter 15. The image of the shepherd who searches for his sheep that was lost has a great impact on children. For the little child this parable offers yet another proof of the Good Shepherd's infinite love.

In the parable of the found sheep children find the uniquely personal and intimate relationship they most hunger for. "He is just for me! He is just for me!" exclaimed Alfonsito, a Mexican boy who had not been accepted by his family on account of his illness. It is especially when children are in a situation of suffering that they identify with the sheep the Good Shepherd embraces in his arms and rests on his shoulders. In the drawings of children who are hospitalized, sometimes for serious illness, it is significant to see that they draw the sheep in such large proportions.

Young children need the protective quality of love. They are also at the stage when their personalities are being formed through a series of relationships. Both vital needs are fulfilled in these two parables.

The Good Shepherd image resonates so deeply within young children that it recalls to them the protection of the maternal womb. This is often expressed in the children's words as well as in their drawings. The message of the parable is so powerful that it can help a young child recapture lost peace, as the following account from an experienced colleague relates:

Cleveland, Ohio

Michael was about three and a half when he entered our Montessori school. He had big blue eyes, a wonderful smile and a likeable personality. He was already familiar with the school and the teacher since his older brother had also attended it and Michael often accompanied him to school, and sometimes stayed to visit. He came from a loving, nurturing family, so we expected smooth sailing for Michael when he came to school. He seemed eager to come and we were eager to have him as part of our community.

Michael's entry into school was anything but smooth. In fact, it was really stormy. He was fine while his mother was at school during the orientation, but as soon as Michael was expected to be in school on his own he had real problems. He cried everyday. Some days it would be on arrival, other days it would begin shortly after arrival. At first the children were concerned about him. They would come and tell me "Michael's crying" as if to say "You must do something about it." After several weeks this was changed to "Oh no! Here goes Michael again." In the meanwhile, I was trying everything in my bag of tricks for helping children to overcome their separation difficulties, but nothing was working. I had daily conversations with his mother to try to determine what might be causing this. There were circumstances in his home life that could be causing some difficulties. His father's job was in jeopardy. An older aunt was dying of cancer and he was very attached to her. We concluded that all this was perhaps just too much for him. I recalled the Good Shepherd parable. Was it too early to tell Michael? Certainly three-year-olds don't recognize that they are the sheep. But then, what did I have to lose? I decided to present the parable and material to him.

The next day I told Michael I had something special I wanted to show him. I took him all alone to one corner of the room and made the presentation to him. It was unbelievable to see how involved Michael became and much to my utter dismay, I realized Michael recognized that he was a sheep. It was nothing I had done.

That day Michael did not cry at all. It seemed like I was witnessing a miracle. We were out in the playground when Michael's mother arrived to take him home. I signalled to her that it had been a good day while Michael ran to his mother saying, "Mommy, mommy! I didn't cry today!" His mother looked at me questioningly (Is there such a word?) and I just nodded my head to tell her Michael was telling the truth.

When Michael got in the car he said to his mother, "Well, aren't you going to ask me why I didn't cry?" She was a really good mother and knew children, and said, "Well Michael, if you want to tell me, yes I'd like to know." (She later told me that she was dying to know why, but was almost afraid to ask). Michael then replied, "I don't ever have to be afraid again, because I have the Good Shepherd to take care of me."

There was a postscript to this account. Not only was that day "the beginning of the end of Michael's problems at school," but when his aunt died Michael was able to face the event with serenity.

In the next chapter we will outline how to offer the proclamation of the Good Shepherd, based on an approach that has proven helpful to children. The presentation is not only to indicate the process in sharing the parable with children but also to invite you to enjoy its message yourselves. Before doing so, it is timely to mention two factors which enable these parables' life-giving effect to continue throughout the child's growing years.

THE PARABLE'S AFFECTIVE IMPACT

The affective dimension of the Good Shepherd image is so rich that it reflects all the relationships in the child's life. While we avoid asking children personal questions, we made this one exception: "Is there anyone who makes you think of the Good Shepherd?" We have asked many children and the most frequent responses are "Mommy," then "Mommy and Daddy," and all the people they love—the "friend," "teacher," and so on. The children find in the Good Shepherd all the various affective nuances; it is not limited just to one person. One child's response to this question was, "my little sister." This was puzzling. If the special bond comes from the fact that the child is known and protected by the Good Shepherd, it was difficult to understand how a younger sister could give the same safe feeling the Good Shepherd gives. This child's answer became understandable when a psychologist explained it is love that reassures and makes us feel safe, even if it comes from a younger sister.

This may be an indication not to stress only the image of God as Father. If the child does not have a good relationship with his or her father, what can it mean? If we tell them God is the Good Shepherd, then the children themselves can choose the person with whom they have the best relationship. The deepest need in young children is to be in relationship and they discover in the Good Shepherd that Someone with whom to establish a relationship (in listening to his voice), Someone who gives them love and to whom they can give their love. The fact that the Good Shepherd calls each sheep by name has the greatest impact for young children (rather than giving his life for the sheep).

THE PARABLE'S DOCTRINAL CONTENT

The Good Shepherd parable is one of the most important Christological parables; it has a profound doctrinal content. Its doctrinal message is as great as its affective resonance. This parable achieves a perfect balance between knowing and feeling, between the intellectual and emotional aspects of its meaning.

This parable contains the essential core of the Christian message: in the Good Shepherd's self-giving love we find the heart of Christ's paschal mystery, His dying and rising. The deep and living way in which this parable takes root in children confirms that the greatest realities should be given to the smallest ones.

This parable is so vital for children that it becomes the point of reference for all the other themes they know. In their drawings they connect the parable with the resurrection of Christ, with his birth, with the Mass and Baptism. For example, there are drawings done at Christmas in which the infant Christ has become the Good Shepherd.

It is important to note here that connections like this are not presented to the children. We simply give them one theme after another and the connections arise from the children themselves. This means the parable is so much a part of them that they can apply it in a variety of situations. If we learn something only in an academic manner, we know it only in that context but we are unable to transfer it to another situation. If the message has really gone down deep into us, then we can apply it to different areas. It is quite clear that the Good Shepherd is not merely a scholastic subject children have learned. The child's capacity to be in love with God has its roots in this parable. Children truly enjoy the presence of the Good Shepherd in their life.

GROWING WITH THE GOOD SHEPHERD

The richness of this parable is so great that it develops along with the child. As the child grows, the parable will reveal in a gradual manner the other aspects it contains.

- For the child after the age of six it will communicate not only the love that nurtures and protects but also the love that forgives. The special aspect for children from six to ten years of age is that the Good Shepherd looks for the lost sheep, that Jesus' love for us is unchanging. God's unfailing love is what children of this age really need. When we speak with children of this age about God's faithful love, we sense the same kind of enjoyment when we talk with the little ones of the shepherd who "calls by name."

- In preadolescence or the early stage of adolescence it will be the shepherd as guide, his role as leader, that is most striking. Children around the age of ten are drawn to the aspect of the shepherd's "leading" and their "following"; the shepherd walks ahead of the sheep and so the sheep go where the shepherd goes. The shepherd is risen, but he reached the resurrection by passing through death, that is, going through difficulties. Children of this age are beginning to be very enthusiastic about great ideals. This is an heroic ideal that is nourishing for their inner life.

Little by little, the parable accompanies the child through the various phases of growth, always continuing to enrich each developmental stage. The Good Shepherd image touches children so profoundly that it builds their relationship with God on the foundation of enjoyment. And what should religious education be if not a help to enjoy, with wonder and gratitude, the immense richness that the person of God is in our life?

6. PRESENTING THE GOOD SHEPHERD TO CHILDREN

The outline for presenting the Good Shepherd parables (John 10 and Luke 15) follows the way we present parables to children in general. The parts of the presentation are listed in numerical order for the sake of clarity:

1. Telling the parable to the children;
2. Listening and reflecting together;
3. Proclaiming God's Word;
4. Presenting the materials;
5. Praying together;
6. Inviting the children's responses.

It must be emphasized that this is *not* proposed as a hard and fast structure to be rigidly followed. Rather, it is suggested as a sequence of elements conducive to calling forth the child's response to God's Word. While the order may vary slightly, these are the elements basic to presenting children themes from both the Bible and liturgy.

Since this sequence is also applicable to the parables of the kingdom (which we address in the next chapter), each of the six parts will be discussed in detail. These different parts will be highlighted with reference to a) our role in the process of proclamation and b) with some indicators as to presenting the parable to the children.

1. TELLING THE PARABLE

First, tell the parable to the children in your own words, keeping close to the parable as it is written in the Gospel. We need to be careful about our language with children; as far as possible, use the actual words of Scripture.

The more faithful we are to the biblical text the better it is for children. Children like only the simple and most essential.

GOOD SHEPHERD PARABLE

When we tell the parable of the Good Shepherd in our own words, we follow St. John's Gospel (chapter ten) very closely. Although we do not usually alter anything the Scripture text contains, we make these exceptions and omit:

- the verses which refer to the hired hand and wolf for young children;
- the image of the "gate," in order to concentrate on the one image of the Shepherd (two images at the same time would be overwhelming for children);
- the first verses of the parable which speak of the "thief" and "brigand." To understand these first verses, it is necessary to know something about the historical situation in which Jesus spoke. This is not possible to do with children under six years of age. Therefore we do not start with the first words of the parable but begin with the words, "The Good Shepherd calls his sheep by their name."

FOUND SHEEP PARABLE

Perhaps the most obvious message of this parable for us is the moral aspect (sin and conversion) and the revelation of God's forgiving love. However, it is important to say that the aspect of God's love the young child seeks is protective love and this is the *only* perspective in which we tell the parable.

TELLING THE PARABLE TO THE CHILD(REN): PUTTING IT TOGETHER

To give you an idea of how to go about telling these parables to children, we would say (more or less) something like this:

People wanted to be near Jesus. They followed him. They were very attracted by what he said. They wondered to themselves "Who is he?" because he was like everybody else, but he spoke in such a special way. People were very curious about him.

Once, when Jesus wanted to tell them who he was, he began by saying, "I am the Good Shepherd." Maybe he stressed the word *good*. He was not just any shepherd, but the Good Shepherd. The Good Shepherd knows all his sheep by their names. Even though he has many, many sheep, he still knows each one by its name.

The sheep begin to recognize his voice and to listen to him. A bond is created between the shepherd who knows them by their name and the sheep who listen to his voice. He guides them to good pastures. He walks ahead of them, to protect and defend them if there is any danger. They follow him because they know his voice. They would not follow a stranger.

The Good Shepherd gives his life for his sheep. He defends his sheep, even with his life.

He loves his sheep so much that if there is one that does not come back to the sheepfold, the shepherd cannot rest. He must go and look for it. He makes sure that the other sheep are safe, then he goes out to look for the lost sheep. He calls it because he knows it by name. He calls louder and louder perhaps. At last the sheep recognizes the voice of the Good Shepherd and turns towards him. Once again they are together. They are happy to be together.

What does the shepherd do? He lifts the sheep, placing it on his shoulders. The sheep is not tired any more because the shepherd carries it. Now it is as if the sheep was as strong as the shepherd. The sheep can go where the shepherd goes. They return to the sheepfold. They are so happy, they are all so happy.

The voice of the Good Shepherd reaches very, very far. There are so many sheep. There are also some sheep who do not yet belong to his sheepfold. But the Shepherd knows every one by name. Little by little all these other sheep will turn towards him too, and little by little all the sheep will come to him. Then there will be only one flock and only one shepherd.

You can see that we do not present the parable of the found sheep from a moral point of view. In our telling, the children hear and receive its message as another instance of the Good Shepherd's boundless love for them.

2. LISTENING AND REFLECTING TOGETHER

After telling the children the parable in your own words, then begin to reflect on the parable together. Reflecting on the biblical text with children helps them understand that there is something hidden to look for in the parable. A parable is not just a little story; we have to look through it to know what Jesus actually wanted to say.

This is a time of listening *together*, a meditation time for us and for children. When we reflect together with children, it helps them learn how to meditate by themselves. The parables and their meanings can not be exhausted. Children may be meeting the parable for the first time, or they may have already listened to it many times, nevertheless, there is always something new to find in it.

The parable usually portrays two points or levels of reality, one from daily life and one from the transcendent level. The parable unexpectedly puts together these two generally distant points, and invites us to understand why. These two points guide us in our meditation with children. We go back and forth from one point to the other—the everyday and the transcendent—offering reflections and inviting the children to dwell on what the parable is saying to them. This creates the context for discovery; that is, to help children understand there is something for them to discover in the parable.

It is the nature of the parable to leave the door open to further exploration. This is the time to help the children explore its meaning in a meditative spirit. If we say to children "This is the meaning..." by words or attitude, they will stop looking for anything else. Then the parable becomes something already done in a sense; however, a parable always remains open to deeper reflection.

One way to assist children to go more deeply into the parable is to guide them by using many "question marks," as it were, and without any "periods," in order to invite their participation and response. This openness on our part stirs their capacity for reflection and engages their intellectual faculties of imagination and intuition.

GOOD SHEPHERD PARABLE

These reflective questions are gentle and open-ended kinds of stirrings for meditation. They give the child an opportunity to enjoy going over the many ways the shepherd cares for and loves his sheep.

Here are some points for guiding the young child's exploration of the parable:

- The Good Shepherd knows every one of his sheep by name. Gradually the sheep come to recognize his voice, and they listen to it.

- The Good Shepherd leads his sheep out of the sheepfold and he guides them. He walks ahead of his sheep to defend them from every danger.

- The Good Shepherd's love for his sheep is so great that it is like the love that binds together the Father and the Son (in the secret life of the Trinity, verses 14-15).

- The Good Shepherd gives himself to his sheep in many ways (this does not relate only to the moment of death but also to the continuous self-giving of the shepherd's love). He cares for, protects, and defends the flock that belongs to him.

- The Good Shepherd's voice is so powerful that it will reach all the sheep, even those that are not yet a part of his flock, until at last there will be only one flock and one shepherd.

FOUND SHEEP PARABLE

Points for guiding children through this parable are:

- The Good Shepherd knows his sheep so well that if only *one* is missing he must go in search of it.
- The Good Shepherd loves his sheep so much that he cannot bear that even one of them is far away and defenseless.
- He goes to search for it until he finds it.
- When he finds his sheep he is filled with joy. He lifts the sheep onto his shoulders and carries it safely back to the sheepfold.
- They all rejoice together.

REFLECTING TOGETHER WITH THE CHILD(REN): PUTTING IT TOGETHER

The purpose of this reflective moment is to evoke the child(ren)'s own response. In an attempt to convey to you this inviting attitude with the child(ren), the following reflections are put in an open-ended form.

The focal point in this particular meditation with children is to help them understand who the sheep are but without telling them. There is no sense of hurry to arrive at the discovery "I am a sheep," as this is not obvious to the child and takes time. Simply offer reflections such as:

- "Who can the sheep be...?
- They must be so precious to the shepherd...
- He gives his own life for them...
- He looks for them...
- He knows each by its name...."

(That he knows each by name is the most striking detail for children, even more than he gives his life for us.)

- "Do you think these are the same type of sheep as we see in the fields...?"

At times the children will say simply "yes," but continue gently:

- "Do you think so...?
- I am not so sure...
- They are so precious to the shepherd...
- Maybe they are something or someone more important...?"

This may be sufficient for this moment. We never tell the children who the sheep are because that would prevent children from enjoying the discovery. It is wonderful when they realize who the sheep really are; joy is so apparent in them.

Other times there are children who understand immediately; they say something like, "They are not real sheep. We are the sheep." Even if they reach this point right away our reflection has just started. Yes, they may have understood it, but it needs to go deeper into their heart. So we gently return to the details of the parable:

- "So you think we are the sheep...?
- We are so many, yet he knows each of us by our name...?
- Then we are so loved...?
- We are cared for in that way...!"

This allows the children to savor and personalize the parable's message.

3. PROCLAIMING GOD'S WORD: LISTENING TO THE GOSPEL

When you announce the actual Gospel text of the parable to the child(ren), read the biblical text slowly and reverently. At times, also light candles to give an added atmosphere of solemnity.

GOOD SHEPHERD PARABLE: FOR THE YOUNG CHILDREN

Here are the verses of the Good Shepherd parable we announce to *young children* (choose the translation of this text you prefer):

ST. JOHN'S GOSPEL, CHAPTER 10, VERSES:

(3b) The good shepherd calls his own sheep by name and leads them out.

(4) When he has brought out all his own, he goes ahead of them, and the sheep follow him because they know his voice.

(5) They will not follow a stranger, but they will run from him because they do not know the voice of strangers.

(10b) I came that they may have life, and have it abundantly.

(11) I am the good shepherd. The good shepherd lays down his life for the sheep.

(14) I am the good shepherd. I know my own and my own know me,

(15) just as the Father knows me and I know the Father. And I lay down my life for the sheep.

(16) I have other sheep that do not belong to this fold. I must bring them also, and they will listen to my voice. So there will be one flock, one shepherd.

(New Revised Standard Version)

GOOD SHEPHERD PARABLE: FOR THE OLDER CHILDREN

With older children, we include the following two verses as well:

(12) The hired hand, who is not the shepherd and does not own the sheep, sees the wolf coming and leaves the sheep and runs away—and the wolf snatches them and scatters them.

(13) The hired hand runs away because a hired hand does not care for the sheep.

FOUND SHEEP PARABLE

ST. LUKE'S GOSPEL, CHAPTER 15, VERSES:

(4) Which one of you, having a hundred sheep and losing one of them, does not leave the ninety-nine in the wilderness and go after the one that is lost until he finds it?

(5) When he has found it, he lays it on his shoulders and rejoices.

(6) And when he comes home, he calls together his friends and neighbors, saying to them, "Rejoice with me, for I have found my sheep that was lost."

The sequence of presenting the parable has two major segments. Up to this point we have discussed the first, when we speak, listen, and help the child to reflect on the Word of God. Now begins the second segment, the time when the child's listening becomes an *interior listening*. To help the child's own personal listening, we present the materials relating to the parable and then provide an opportunity for activity with them.

4. PRESENTING THE MATERIALS FOR THE PARABLE

Our experience led us to seek a means of assisting children during the time of inner listening, in an indirect manner, so that their relationship with God can be established. This is the aim of the materials and the reason why we offer them to children at this moment in the presentation.

Our materials for the parables (as for other themes of the message) are very simple. They are composed of the most important elements of the biblical or liturgical text and nothing more. The point of the parable is to make an invisible reality concrete for us; we have further concretized this in materials, it is that simple! (Our Good Shepherd materials are made in wood. There is a green circular base for the pasture on which is a fenced-in area for the sheepfold; there is a shepherd figure, and sheep figures. These have not needed repainting even though, across the many years, they have passed through hundreds of children's hands. This shows the care and respect with which children work with them.)

PRESENTING THE MATERIAL TO THE YOUNG CHILDREN: PUTTING IT TOGETHER

After reading the Gospel text we show the children these materials.

We read (or re-tell) the text again and move the wooden figures. We have to be careful about our movements as children are most interested in movement. For example, it may be spontaneous for us to move a number of sheep at a time, instead we take them one after the other and move them slowly and carefully. The following is to give you an idea of the movements involved:

- "The Shepherd calls the sheep by their name and the sheep come into the sheepfold."

  (Put out the shepherd figure, then place the sheep one at a time into the sheepfold.)

- "The sheep are safe and happy in the sheepfold with their Shepherd. The Shepherd guides them out and walks ahead of them."

  (Move the sheep out of the fold slowly, putting them one after another behind the shepherd.)

- "The sheep listen to the Shepherd's voice and follow him. He shows them the path. He walks ahead of them and guides them to the good pasture."

  (Shepherd figure leads, with sheep following.)

We have put the words and movements on different lines to show the importance of separating the words and movements into distinct parts (rather than speaking and moving the figures at the same time).

PRESENTING THE MATERIAL TO THE OLDER CHILDREN

For children *six years of age and older*, we include the figures of the hired hand and the wolf. As an indication of what to say and how to move the figures, we would do something to this effect:

- "The hired man is one who does not care for the sheep."

  (Remove the shepherd figure. Put out the figure of the hired man.)

- "If the wolf comes, the hired man runs away because he cares only about himself."

  (Put out the wolf figure. Then remove the figure of the hired man.)

Then we return the figure of the Good Shepherd and place it in front of the sheep:

- "If the wolf comes, the Shepherd gives his life for the sheep."

  (Remove the wolf figure.)

Sometimes we may lay the shepherd figure down at this point. A child may question, "But if the shepherd has fallen, who can protect the sheep?" This is an opportune moment to recall with the children who the shepherd truly is. We would speak along these lines:

- Jesus is not just any shepherd.

- He is the "Good Shepherd."

- Jesus gives his life for us.

- He died, but what happened afterwards?

- Jesus is risen and lives again.

(Standing the Good Shepherd figure in an upright position) we continue:

- "Jesus died, he is risen and lives again. He is always leading his flock and protecting them."

This is a wonderful opportunity to proclaim the resurrection.

5. PRAYING TOGETHER

Everything described to this point is intended to create an atmosphere conducive to prayer. Our listening with children—in speaking together, reading, and retelling God's Word through the concrete materials—all unfolds in a prayerful manner. Therefore, presenting the materials may be an especially appropriate time to invite the child's own response in prayer.

These parables fill the children with wonder and joy. There are many prayers in which the children pour out their joy. For instance, a group of children were very moved at hearing the parable, so their catechist invited them, "Would you like to go to the chapel now to say something to the Good Shepherd?" As the catechist was putting things in order before leaving for the chapel, the children had left on their own, without any noise. They prayed for a while and then they returned to their room. Later one of the children came over and confided to the catechist, "Do you know what I told Him? 'You are good, because you guide us with goodness.'"

6. INVITING THE CHILDREN'S RESPONSES

Thus far we have initiated the meditation process, listened to God's Word, presented the materials, and perhaps spent some time in prayer together. Now we make the materials available for the children's activity. The materials offer them a means of remaining with and going more deeply into the theme presented.

To help children to continue reflecting, we do not need to be directly present, so we can step aside. We put the materials at their disposal to use by themselves. There are many different kinds of activity children do with these in response. For instance, if they can read, one child may read the parable/scripture booklet while another child moves the figures. Or, if they cannot read, they tell the parable to themselves. This can be more interesting!

If we are given to hear some of their words or observe their way of doing things, we will appreciate even more how valuable the child's own activity really is. During the time children are on their own, they are absorbing and internalizing the parable; their activity can be a passage to prayer or prayer itself.

IN THEIR OWN WAY

An incident that illustrates the value of the child's way of being and doing happened while a catechist was observing a young boy who was working with the Good Shepherd materials on his own. First he put the shepherd outside the sheepfold, then he had the sheep follow after the shepherd. Before the child moved a sheep, he turned around the shepherd figure to face the sheep and then turned it back towards the gate. The child repeated this each time he moved a sheep out of the sheepfold. After the child had finished with the materials and returned them to their place, the catechist approached the child gently and said, "May I ask you something?" When the child nodded, the catechist inquired, "Why did the shepherd turn towards the sheep so many times?" And the little boy responded, "Because he calls them by their names." He had been so struck by this detail that he repeated the gesture for every sheep.

IN THEIR OWN WORDS

During the children's personal activity with the materials, they are able to apply the parable to their own life. An example of this involved a young child whose school was in a suburb where the railway tracks passed by. The railway was so close it presented a danger, and the children were told constantly to be careful and not go near it. While this little boy was working with the Good Shepherd material, he put all the sheep into the sheepfold except one, the "lost" sheep. He placed this one far from the rest and then started speaking to it: "Where are you going? You're crazy! Don't you know it's dangerous?" Afterwards, he moved the shepherd over to the sheep, put the sheep with the shepherd figure, and returned them to the sheepfold together.

This shows the importance of giving children the time and the means for their own response, for this is when and how it becomes a part of their life. This does not refer only to the materials we present but also to other forms of the child's personal, creative work, of which art activity is one example.

ART RESPONSE

For instance, we mentioned that the children often realize who the sheep really are only after our time of reflecting with them. Many times we finish this meditative moment and not one child has understood the real identity of the sheep. Then, little by little, during their self-chosen activity, they make their own discovery. This was especially clear in the case of one boy who drew the figure of a shepherd, many sheep each with a heart above it, and two children among the sheep. When he brought the drawing for the catechist to look at, she asked, "Why have you drawn those two children?" The child answered, "Because *while I was working* I understood that we are the sheep." The child had not understood while he was with the catechist and the other children but only later, during his own personal dialogue with the inner Teacher.

Another example is the drawing made by a young girl who lives in an institute. In the center of the page she drew a red heart and wrote inside it "happy heart." Then she drew an altar with candles, a few sheep holding little candles, and also children. She printed on her drawing the words "children have the light" and "Mommy, I love you," though she hardly knew her mother. As the girl was doing this, the catechist noticed she had drawn a house and later transformed it into a church; afterwards her catechist asked, "Why have you changed it?" and the little girl said, "Because the house of the sheep is the church." How impressive that "happy heart" is! The affective richness of the parable is so great that it actually brings joy to a child who is almost abandoned by her parents.

SUMMARY

This way of presenting the parables is a process of proclamation that helps children know the parable in more than an academic or cognitive sense. There are two ways of knowing things: we may know and remember many things because of the effort we made to learn them, such as in passing examinations. There are other things that we know yet we may neither be aware of nor remember where they came from; they are in us, part of us. This approach to announcing God's Word helps children know this parable in this second way.

There was a conversation between two women, one who was in her early 20's and the other who had been her catechist when she was a young child. As the younger woman was recalling what she remembered of their days together in the catechetical center, she asked her former catechist: "But...you didn't present the Good Shepherd to me." The catechist, remembering quite well that she had, asked her, "But you know it don't you?" "Of course I do!" she responded immediately. What was interesting was that the young woman could not recall the first time she had been presented this parable. It was so deeply rooted in her that it was as if she had always known the Good Shepherd.

SUMMARY

7. THE MYSTERY OF LIFE: PARABLES OF THE KINGDOM

Let us recall two characteristics or capacities of young children. The first is the young child's capacity to take hold of life and become involved in it in a whole-person way. The second is the young child's capacity to see reality and to penetrate beyond the visible and the tangible.

THE CHILD'S CALL

These two abilities are telling us something. In these we hear a silent call on the part of the young child: Help me to contemplate the miracle of life.

This call means that a deep and delicate service is being asked of us. The young child needs our help to gaze upon the world and all of creation, and to probe it to its depths.

We are asked to help young children behold with wonder the miracle of life in itself so that they become able to see its reflections in persons and things. To do this we have the wealth of Gospel parables to assist us and provide us with the instruments we need. The parables of the kingdom are the key which the young child uses to open the door to this miracle of life, in particular these five:

- The parable of the mustard seed
  (Gospel of St. Matthew, Chapter 13, verses 31–32);

- The parable of the yeast
  (Gospel of St. Matthew, Chapter 13, verse 33);

- The parable of the seed of grain
  (Gospel of St. Mark, Chapter 4, verses 26–28);

- The parable of the pearl
  (Gospel of St. Matthew, Chapter 13, verses 45–46);

- The parable of the hidden treasure
  (Gospel of St. Matthew, Chapter 13, verse 44).

FOOD FOR THE FUTURE

These parables, given in early childhood, not only nurture the young child's needs but they have a future value as well, since they prepare the child to read the many elements of reality in a special light in later childhood. The special ability of the young child is to perceive life by probing to its depths. In later childhood, the child's eyes see life's widening horizons and the numerous aspects they reveal. When the young child is helped to grasp the religious meaning of life in its wholeness, then it will be possible in later childhood for the child also to read the many signs of creation in a religious key as well.

This becomes clearer in reference to two characteristics of older children (beyond the age of six or seven) mentioned earlier:

1)   The horizons and interests of the child broaden around six years of age. Therefore, reading the various details of life is the focus of the older child after the age of six.

2)   At this time the frontiers of reality expand before the older child's gaze, but life also becomes more fragmented. This is why older children need a global view of life because it helps them to discover that there is a deep and unified root to all the different aspects of reality.

It is important that the older child reaches this moment prepared, because it is from a foundation of global love for life that each and every manifestation of life—in relation to people and things—will be colored with love. The child, after the age of six, will be able to love all life's many aspects because life as a whole has become visible as a mysterious gift, a gift that is both within us and surrounding us.

Helping older children to read the various creation signs becomes a life-giving exploration when they *already* have an inner key they can use to interpret them. If we were to diagram the inner movements of the spirit, as it were, we would say:

Early Childhood (six years of age and under)	**Older Childhood** (seven to ten years of age or so)
from the global view of life as a whole	to the particular view of life in its many details
from the essential	to the secondary

Following this direction helps

■   the young child to go to the core of reality;

■   and prepares the child to read the signs of creation in later life.

The key will be present already in the child's own heart.

THE PARABLES OF THE KINGDOM OF GOD

These parables of the kingdom of God, that cause children's eyes to shine with light and to glow with wonder, will be grouped into two sections. The first are three parables that reveal the mystery of the kingdom's growth and power. The second group is composed of two parables that reveal the beauty and value of the kingdom of God. Grouping the parables in this way allows us to discuss some aspects they have in common when reflecting on them with children.

THE PARABLES OF THE SEEDS AND YEAST

There are the parables that show the kingdom as something very small, so tiny that it almost escapes our notice and yet which becomes, so incredibly, something very great.

In the following three parables, the Gospel invites us to dwell on the mystery of the kingdom in two different moments—the beginning and concluding moments—and places before us the staggering contrast between something extremely small and something great. Even more extraordinary is the fact that the great comes from the little, the less becomes the more.

■   The Gospel speaks to us of the mustard seed. It is the smallest of all seeds no bigger than the head of a pin, and yet it becomes a tree where the birds of the air come to make their nests (Matthew 13:31–32).

> The kingdom of heaven is like a mustard seed that someone took and sowed in his field; it is the smallest of all the seeds, but when it has grown it is the greatest of shrubs and becomes a tree, so that the birds of the air come and make nests in its branches.

■   The Gospel tells us about a woman who mixes three measures of flour with yeast until all the dough is leavened. The yeast changes the small lump of flour into a large loaf of bread (Matthew 13:33).

> The kingdom of heaven is like yeast that a woman took and mixed in with three measures of flour until all of it was leavened.

■   No less astonishing is the parable of that seed of grain the farmer sows in the ground; it sprouts and grows, he knows not how (Mark 4:26–28).

> The kingdom of God is as if someone would scatter seed on the ground, and would sleep and rise night and day, and the seed would sprout and grow, he does not know how. The earth produces of itself, first the stalk, then the head, then the full grain in the head.

All three parables show us the beginning and ending moments of a process, without lingering over the development that happens in between. This highlights the contrast between the tiny and the great, and the great that comes forth from the tiny.

In fact, so wonderful is the growth of life that we cannot grasp it during its process of unfolding; it captures our attention when it is already complete in some sense. This inspires awe. We all have felt wonder at seeing the first budding of a branch that just a day earlier seemed dead and lifeless. We have experienced the surprise at the change, so sudden it seems to us, of a field that is transformed from its winter state to put on the face of Spring.

PRESENTING THESE PARABLES TO THE CHILDREN

Since the approach to presenting these parables of the kingdom follows the same sequence outlined for the Good Shepherd parable, we will concentrate only on some points for helping children to listen and reflect on the parable (the meditative moment in the presentation with children).

LISTENING AND REFLECTING WITH THE CHILDREN

In reflecting on these parables with the children, the main thrust is to help the children to dwell in a restful state of wonder. But it does not stop there.

The seeds and the leaven become our starting point and springboard for guiding the children to the deepest level of life so that together we can begin to understand its universal meaning.

The following are a few general guiding points for listening to and meditating on these parables.

■   In each case begin with the actual element, the mustard seed or a seed of grain or the tiny yeast. (These parables are offered one at a time to the child and with sufficient—even lengthy—intervals of time between them to allow each to be savored fully.)

■ How extremely small it is (especially the mustard seed)! Yet it grows and becomes bigger! How does this happen?

■ Help the child to see that this same marvelous activity is happening throughout the entire world by calling attention to the fact that there is a power at work in the universe which is greater than whatever is before us and whatever we can perceive about it.

This process of reflection leads the child to discover that there is a secret unfolding: in the whole of creation—going from a littleness without measure to the greatest of realities—there is an energy at work which is beyond every capacity of the human person.

THE KINGDOM OF GOD AND THE MUSTARD SEED

To give a more concrete example of how the children may be directed towards this sense of discovery, here are some specific reflections relating to the mustard seed parable. In your meditation with the children, the following aspects may be highlighted:

■ We are able to make big things by putting many small things together (for instance, by building a house with many bricks);

■ but none of us knows how to make one small thing into a great thing.

We are unable to do this because when such a change takes place—as happens with the growing seed—it has been caused by the power of life itself, and we know, as human creatures, that we are not the masters of life, nor can we control life.

Continue your reflection by helping the children to see:

■ that the life-giving breath that fills the tiny mustard seed and makes it grow big is the breath that is within everything that is created;

■ that small seed, so little that it gets lost in the palm of our hand, lets us see the world around us in a different way, and it becomes gradually transparent. There is an immense power working there, acting within the whole of creation, causing it to go always towards the more—more life.

Direct the child's attention now to the fact that we can see that same mysterious power, which is at work in the entire universe, is present and working in us as well:

■ "Can we see this happening in us too...?

■ Look how long your arms and legs are...

■ How much bigger your body is now than the day you were born...

■ How different you are now than when you were a little baby...

■ Then you were unable to move by yourself...now you are someone who can move, jump, do lots of things...now you know so many things!

■ How you are changing...you can see it in the abilities developing every day in yourself...

■ How did all this happen...?"

This approach helps the children discover that we too are involved in this marvelous movement that goes—wonderfully!—towards more and more life. It is a dynamism we are incapable of dominating.

THE MYSTERY OF LIFE

These parables introduce children to the mystery of life itself, in all its greatness, beyond our ability to understand completely. They come to the awareness that the mysterious power we are able to catch sight of in the tiny mustard seed is in ourselves too. Can we call it ours? Yes and no: it is within us, since we can see it working in ourselves, but we cannot control it. As the Gospel asks: Can any of us add "a single hour" to our life? (Matthew 6:27).

These parables bring us in touch with the existence of a powerful force that involves the entire world and which moves within us as well, and yet it does not come from us. To whom does it belong? We are brought face to face with the evidence that life is a gift which has been given to us. We may call it ours in so far as we receive it, but it does not have its source in us.

MYSTERY OF DEATH

The parables of the seeds and the yeast, which introduce children to the mystery of life, also help us approach the mystery of death.

For instance, we can reflect with children in the following ways:

- Up to a certain point in our lives we witness the presence of a power within us, on the physical level too, which impels us to grow.

- When our bodies have reached their full growth, do we lose this inner force and strength, or does it continue to function in another way?

- From the first moment of life, this inner movement towards the *more* directs us to accomplishments that may not be obvious to our sight but they are extremely real. (These relate to achievements in the field of knowledge and the inner formation of the whole person.)

- In each of us there is an inner dynamism that constantly urges us to become greater. And it is never-ending.

In reflecting along such lines, the child is guided to the awareness that this power is continually at work within us; it does not stop at death. Death is seen, therefore, in the light of a new and more radical passage from the *less* to the *more*.

THE PARABLES OF THE PEARL
AND THE TREASURE

The positive impact of the above parables in children is heightened by the following two parables of the kingdom: the pearl and the treasure. These parables, both found in the thirteenth chapter of Matthew's Gospel, draw children to dwell on the priceless value of God's gift.

- First is the parable of the merchant who goes in search of precious pearls, and when he has found the one of great value, he sells all that he has to buy it (Matthew 13:45–46).

  The kingdom of heaven is like a merchant in search of fine pearls; on finding one pearl of great value, he went and sold all that he had and bought it.

- The other parable is like this. It is about the farmer who, digging in a field, finds a hidden treasure. Joyfully, he too sells what he has so he can buy that field (Matthew 13:44).

  The kingdom of heaven is like treasure hidden in a field, which someone found and hid; then in his joy he goes and sells all that he has and buys that field.

These parables lead to contemplation and to action at the same time. They contain a strong ascetic element, in that both figures in the parables renounce all that they have.

As adults, this is often the element of these parables that strikes us most. However, this is not true for little children, and it is important *not* to emphasize this aspect with them. This aspect of "selling all" responds to the inner attitude of the adolescent or, at the earliest, the pre-adolescent.

PRESENTING THE PARABLES TO THE CHILD(REN)

The principal purpose in reflecting on the parables of the pearl and the treasure, like the other kingdom parables, is to evoke gently the spirit of wonder and awe in little children. They reinforce what the previous parables have helped the children to discover: so great is the value of that kingdom within us and around us that it surpasses everything else.

In listening to these two parables and reflecting on them with young children, there is a single focus:

- the pearl—how beautiful and precious it must be...!

- the hidden treasure—containing who knows how many precious gems...!

- Remember that no attention is given to what must be done to have the pearl and the treasure, since the young child is not yet at the age to be concerned about *doing*.

- Announce this message of the kingdom as food for the child's *being*. This will be expressed later as well in a certain way of living and acting (see Chapter Twelve).

Once again, with a different nuance, these two parables help the child to dwell upon the wonder of the kingdom and to enjoy the great happiness there is in belonging to it.

The parables of the kingdom offer children a proper orientation to reality. In each one of us there is a very great "hidden treasure," an inner wealth, a potential. However, these do not have their origin in us, they are gift. This makes us feel very great and very small at the same time.

These parables establish the foundation for our religious attitude as human creatures. We recognize that God's power is within us, but we realize that it does not come from us. This brings the awareness that we need to go outside and beyond ourselves to find our true origin and source.

8. BAPTISM: THE GIFT OF LIFE

The baptism of infants is a part of the most ancient tradition of the Church. This practice implies a recognition of the child's capacity to live in relationship with God, even from the time of infancy.

LIFE IN ABUNDANCE

The sacrament of Baptism is a living reality, already present and at work within the young child. This sacrament is an active and rich source of abundant life within the child. And children need our help to become aware, as soon as possible, of this immense gift within them. An effective approach in doing this is to introduce the children to the signs associated with baptism.

Religious education gives much time and attention to helping children appreciate the beauty of nature. This is good. However, religious formation of young children can also help them to realize there is a dimension of life that is beyond the limits of what our senses perceive. In the signs of the baptismal rite the child finds an even greater richness, the "hidden treasure." This hidden treasure exists not only in the created world surrounding us but within each one of us as well.

THE SIGNS OF BAPTISM

Traditionally the Church provides us with a way of piercing through the realities whose meaning we cannot grasp by means of our senses alone. Signs speak a language rich in meaning and impact. Children need to be introduced to this language as they would to any other,

- by helping them to become aware of the signs;
- by helping them to read these signs so as to discover their meaning.

Children are able to read these signs because of their capacity to go beyond what is seen and touched to reach the meaning inside. The child, particularly the young child, has a naturally strong interest in everything involving movement and language.

To point out the meaning of these signs, only a *few words* are necessary. The visual language of signs is an impressive and effective means of communicating the message to children. Therefore, let the wordless language speak to the children, taking care not to overpower the visual language with spoken language.

There are many baptismal signs and gestures:

- the Word (the Bible, the Scripture readings);
- the light (the paschal candle representing the Risen Christ and the smaller white candle for the one being baptized);
- the white garment (or robe worn during the rite of baptism);
- the water (blessed in the baptismal font and poured over the child's head);
- the oils (the oil of the catechumens and the aromatic sacred chrism);
- the sign of the cross (done in many forms during the rite).

The major signs associated with baptism are water and light. These two signs have an obvious and powerful natural content, and we can help children to value both as gifts of nature.

In meditating on the water and light, children are eager and ready to take hold of their deeper meaning. One time we were speaking about the light with children, and a little girl said: "It's not light, it's goodness." Another time, when the children were reflecting about the light of baptism and the light of the sun, a five-year-old boy remarked: "This light isn't even like sunlight. The light of the sun is natural, but the light of baptism is..." and here words failed him. But the idea was clear in his mind.

PRESENTING THE BAPTISMAL SIGNS TO THE CHILDREN

THE LIGHT

The season of Easter is an apt time to introduce children to the sacrament of Baptism. One way to begin is by helping them to enter into the meaning of the symbol of light.

Begin the reflection on the gift of baptism by showing the children the paschal candle.

- Light the paschal candle, saying that it is the symbol of the Risen Christ.
- Then invite the children to bring their own candle to light from the paschal candle.
- Recall the children's own baptismal day; this is the day when the light of the Risen Christ came to each one of us. In doing this, the children see for themselves that the light—the life of the Risen Lord—that baptism brings is not something we can give to ourselves. Ponder on this life symbolized by the light, which is a gift, a gift that the Risen Christ gives to each one of us.
- When all our candles are lit, pause for a moment to dwell on the fact that the light shining from the candle in our hands is the same as the light of the paschal candle. This seeing helps the children to discover that the very life of the Risen Christ is in each one of us!

THE WHITE BAPTISMAL GARMENT

Another symbol of baptism, which is linked to the light, is the white garment or robe.

Using an actual baptismal garment if available or a miniature replica of one:

- show the child(ren) the white garment that is worn during the baptismal celebration. This impact of the light is reinforced (since white is the color of light);
- this white robe covered the child at the moment of baptism, showing "on the outside" (as a child once said) that we are truly "children of the light."

THE WATER

At another time the children can be introduced to the gift that baptism is by concentrating on the symbol of water. In reflecting on this sign, help the children to understand:

- that the water of baptism is the same, and not the same as the water we usually use for so many things;
- because in the gift of baptism the water is given to us in the name of the Father and the Son and the Holy Spirit, that is, in the power of the Holy Trinity.

Then, continuing in this meditative spirit:

- do the gesture of pouring the water slowly (into a miniature replica of a baptismal font if possible);
- recall to the children that at this moment during our baptism we were called by name;
- say the child's name, and pour the water slowly;
- while speaking the words: "I baptize you in the name of the Father, and of the Son, and of the Holy Spirit."

During the quiet atmosphere of this moment, the children are able to hear the gentle sound of the water and the words. Being called by name is an element that recalls the parable of the Good Shepherd and has a deep resonance in the children. So much so, that when doing this with a group of children, frequently this action of pouring the water and saying the child's name continues until all the children have been named.

GESTURES OF GIFT

There are also gestures during the rite of baptism which help the children to experience the gift that this sacrament is in our life. The most obvious of these gestures is the sign of the cross.

THE SIGN OF THE CROSS

In reflecting with the children on the meaning of this gesture, highlight some of the ways and times it is seen during the baptismal rite by telling and showing them, for example:

- the child is signed with the cross on the forehead with the thumb;
- the sign of the cross is traced not only on the surface of the skin but it enters deep down into the child's heart, never to be erased.

Let the children see how this sign is used on many other occasions as well:

- in blessing the mother;
- and the father;
- and the whole community;
- and over the child with a large sign of the cross, larger than the child itself, which covers the child "like a shield" (as the children themselves have said, thus echoing the Fathers of the Church without knowing it).

GESTURE OF THE HAND

Another baptismal sign that introduces the children to the mystery and marvel of this abundant life given in baptism, is the gesture of the priest stretching his open hand (the imposition of the hand) over the water in the baptismal font.

- let the children see this gesture by doing it (preferably over a replica—in miniature—of a baptismal font);

- tell the children that there is a beautiful prayer that accompanies this gesture asking the Father to send the Holy Spirit into the water so that it might have the power to give us life.

Children are capable of seeing through this gesture to the meaning it expresses: the power of God. The Holy Spirit is at work in the baptismal water, transforming us and making us sharers in the very life of God.

9. THE EUCHARIST: MEETING THE GOOD SHEPHERD

Are little children capable of taking part in the Eucharist? Or is it perhaps too great a mystery for them? Would it be better to postpone their introduction to and participation in it until a more mature age? Regrettably this was our opinion at one time, until the children taught us differently. The young child goes towards the simple and essential, whereas we were looking for complicated ways. There is nothing more simple or essential in its greatness than the Eucharist.

With the Good Shepherd image we found the way to present the Mass to young children. The children showed us the key to the aspect of the Mass that responded to their needs. It was the children who taught us the simplest way to present it: the Eucharist is the time and place when the Good Shepherd calls his sheep in a most particular way. When we reached this point, it was very beautiful to see that the children reacted as if they had been waiting just for that. The presentation of the Mass as the time and place in which we meet our Good Shepherd in a special way was grasped eagerly, and right away it went very deeply into them.

This is the aspect of the Eucharist that nurtures the needs of young children. Their response to it showed us that the young child needs the heart of the message; it also showed us how difficult it is for us to reach such an essential level!

THE BOND BETWEEN BIBLE AND LITURGY

The presentation we will describe offers the vital link between Scripture and liturgy. In presenting the Mass in this way, the unity between the biblical word and the liturgical action is made visible. The result is that the affective impact of the Good Shepherd parable—so powerful and profound—overflows onto the celebration of the Eucharist as well. Then an "affective integration" (as psychologists call it) occurs in the child; it is an awareness grasped by heart and mind together.

The young child needs to know about the Mass and to understand about the unique relationship it creates between God and the human person. More important, if the child is helped to enjoy this meeting with God, then the Eucharist is experienced in its fullness. The link between the Eucharist and a well-loved parable like the Good Shepherd contributes to the child's enjoyment.

PRESENTING THE EUCHARIST TO THE CHILD(REN)

The parable of the Good Shepherd is a paschal parable: "I lay down my life for the sheep" (John 10:15). This is why it serves as a means for introducing children to the Mass, that action in which Christ's complete self-gift (pasch) is actualized.

The presentation of the Eucharist to children unfolds in two parts. It is accompanied by a very simple type of material. For the first part the materials are:

- Those used in the presentation of the Good Shepherd parable (the green circular, wooden base with a fenced-in fold attached to it and the two-dimensional figures for the shepherd and the sheep);
- another round base made of wood (with a textured green surface, such as felt);
- a miniature table to represent the altar and a white cloth to cover it (before we present this the children have already been introduced to the altar and its related articles, so this is not new for them);
- a small two-dimensional replica of the shepherd figure (usually an image pasted to wood, with a small base so that it can stand upright);
- a miniature chalice and paten (with a replica of bread on it).

For the second part in the presentation on the Eucharist, new figures are added. These are wooden two-dimensional, painted figures to represent people, both adults and children (in sufficient number to substitute all the sheep figures).

PART I. THE EUCHARISTIC PRESENCE OF THE GOOD SHEPHERD

To introduce young children to the Eucharist, the two circular bases are placed side by side, first the one with the sheepfold, sheep and shepherd. The other green, round base is put beside it and then the altar table with cloth is placed on it.

LISTENING AND REFLECTING WITH THE CHILD(REN)

Here are some of the principal points in reflecting with the children:

- The Good Shepherd knows each of his sheep by name. He calls his sheep to a special meeting with him.
- The sheep know the Shepherd's voice and he calls them.
- The Good Shepherd calls his sheep to the altar to be near him.
- The sheep listen to his voice and come.
- They gather around their Good Shepherd at the altar.

This perspective enables the child to see the Eucharist as the *sacrament of the gift*. All that the Shepherd does on behalf of his sheep, which the child has experienced already through the parable, is concretized in this Eucharistic moment.

PRESENTING THE MATERIALS TO THE CHILD(REN)

To offer an indication of the sequence of the first presentation, we would say something like this to the child(ren):

- The Good Shepherd calls the sheep by their name. The Good Shepherd calls his sheep to be with him around the altar.

  (The good shepherd figure is placed in a central position on the altar.)

- The sheep listen and respond to his voice. They gather around him.

  (Move the sheep from the fold and place them around the altar.)

- At Mass, the Good Shepherd is very close to his sheep. When the Good Shepherd calls us around his altar, he is present in the bread and wine.

  (Place the chalice and the paten with bread on the altar.)

- If this image is here or not, it is the same. The Good Shepherd is always with his sheep and the sheep are near their Good Shepherd. So, whether the image is on the altar or not, it does not change anything. The Good Shepherd is here in the bread and wine.

  (Remove the shepherd image.)

This is the first part in the presentation: the Good Shepherd calls his sheep to an encounter with him—a most particular meeting—where he gives himself to them (as seen in the bread and wine). It is important to allow the children adequate time to visualize the sheep around the altar (leave an interval of time before presenting the following part). This helps the affective bond between the parable and the Mass to be established and the affective richness of the parable will be transferred to the Mass.

PART II. THE EUCHARISTIC PRESENCE OF THE GOOD SHEPHERD

At a later time, the second part is presented. During this presentation the children are helped to listen to Jesus' words at the Last Supper, which the celebrant prays during the Mass. These words reveal in an explicit way the total self-gift Jesus offers to us. They also express an invitation, almost an insistent one, for us to accept this gift:

> Take and eat,
>   this is my Body
>   which is given for you.
> Take and drink,
>   this is my Blood
>   which is poured out for you.

PRESENTING THE MATERIALS

Of course, by this time the children know the real identity of the sheep—we are the sheep. After the children have had enough time to visualize and internalize the link between Scripture (parable) and the liturgy (Mass), now is the time to make the passage: the figures of the sheep are substituted with the figures representing people. There is an exchange of the figures. (The figures of the sheep are put away and the figures for the people are placed around the altar.)

When this is completed, the figure representing the priest is placed at the altar:

- There is a sheep called the priest, who has a particular mission: to proclaim the words of Jesus. The priest prays Jesus' words over the bread, "This is my body offered for you" and over the wine, "This is my blood given for you."

At this point the children are looking at this second circular green base (recalling the sheepfold) with people around the altar and also a priest. This is what they see at Mass.

PART III. THE SIGNS OF THE EUCHARIST

The other approach to the Eucharist with young children is through its signs.

A. THE GESTURES OF GIFT

During the celebration of the Mass there are certain signs which express the most profound content of the Eucharist by means of movements or gestures. There are three gestures especially that reveal and reinforce the Eucharist in the light of the sacrament of the gift.

■   The first occurs before the priest prays the words of the Lord at the Last Supper. He opens his hands, places them together, and spreads them over the bread and wine. This gesture of the imposition of the hands is a prayer to invoke the Holy Spirit. Using visual language, the movement of the hands shows us that we are asking for the gift of God's Holy Spirit.

This gesture (known by its Greek name *epiclesis*) illustrates the prayer that accompanies it, in which the Father is asked to send the Holy Spirit to transform the bread and wine into the presence of the Risen Christ. In presenting this gesture to children it helps them see through to the meaning of the hands moving from above to below—the invisible gift that the Father sends us—which the words of Jesus at the Last Supper express.

■   At the conclusion of the Eucharistic prayer, there is another gesture.

This action of the raising of the bread and wine by the priest complements the first movement of the hands. This is the gesture of offering. The gesture of offering, "through Christ, with Christ and in Christ," goes up from us to the Father. It is our way of responding to the gift we have received.

Highlighting these two complementary movements—the hands moving from above and the hands moving from below—helps the child to see the exchange of gifts. These gestures that symbolize an exchange of gifts express the covenant in a visible way: God's self-giving to us, our gift of self to God. The relationship of covenant, God's with us and ours with God, is realized in a most particular way during the Eucharist.

■   In this sacrament of the "new and everlasting covenant," our personal relationship with God is concretized and strengthened, and through God, with every other person as well. Indeed, there is a third gesture that lets us see this horizontal dimension—our relationship with one another—of the covenant. It is called the gesture of peace.

The exchange of peace we share with each other during the Mass expresses in an explicit manner that unique relationship we have, through the one broken bread, with all people of every time and place.

This sign of the exchange of peace enables us to see something like a mysterious thread that knits us all together and unites us in love. It is a gesture which shows in a tangible way that we are bound together with those who are celebrating with us here and now, with those participating in other places as well, and also with those who have shared in the Eucharist in other times too.

Through the sign of peace the children come to see the thread that, bridging time and distance, unites together the Shepherd with the sheep of all times and places.

B. SIGNS AND SYMBOLS

There are other signs and symbols relating to the Mass which capture the interest of little children. When children enter a church or attend the celebration of the Eucharist they see many and various kinds of objects, colors and images. In introducing the children to these and helping them to know their names, use, and meaning, understanding is born.

To do this, there are simple ways of making miniaturized replicas (in paper, wood, or whatever materials you have available) of the following:

- the altar, and the sacred vessels used during the Eucharistic liturgy (paten, chalice, candles, cross);

- replicas of other articles can be gradually added (the book of Scripture readings called the Lectionary, and the lectern; the cruets for the water and wine; the various altar cloths and so forth);

- objects associated with the sanctuary (tabernacle and sanctuary lamps, etc.);

- the vestments of the priest (first the chasuble is presented, and later the other vestments, such as the alb, stole and cincture).

The purpose of telling the children the names of these and showing their use is to familiarize them with the objects and symbols they have seen at Mass, but perhaps without knowing what they were seeing. Frequently, parents will remark how their child will point out with delight, "There is the altar," and so on. The child's eagerness to know new words and their ease in saying them is a reflection of their naturally keen interest in everything associated with language.

As the children gradually learn the names and meaning of all the articles associated with the liturgy of the Word and the Eucharistic liturgy, their enjoyment of and participation in the Mass increases.

C. COLORS

The colors—there are four primarily—which are used during liturgical celebrations have a symbolic meaning which catch the child's attention. Introducing children to their names and meaning helps them to understand and identify the different liturgical seasons during the year.

- Purple is the color that signifies the time of preparing and getting ready to celebrate a great feast. Purple is used during the four weeks of Advent before the feast of Christmas, and during the six weeks of Lent preceding the greatest of feasts, Easter.

- White is the color used when we are actually celebrating the feast itself; for example, for the Christmas season and for the seven weeks of the Easter season.

- Red is especially for Pentecost, the feast of the Holy Spirit.

- The color green is used for the time following these feasts, during the time when these great feasts are, so to speak, growing in us.

Colors are a key to many activities relating to:

- liturgical seasons;

- the vestments the celebrant wears during the celebrations (small models of these can be made in paper or cloth);

- the decorations of the church (altar cloths, tabernacle veil, for instance), as well as flowers, liturgical art, and so forth.

Many opportunities for activity can be offered using the simplest of materials. For example:

- a pre-cut collage of the articles used during the Mass, which the child pastes in place;

- pictures of the vestments or the sacred objects of the altar and sanctuary for young children to paste, trace, or draw on their own.

10. CELEBRATING LIFE: CHRISTMAS AND EASTER

To help young children to celebrate the feasts of Christmas and Easter, our aim has been, above all, to lead them to Scripture. The Gospels are the source, a wellspring, overflowing with living waters.

NEWS OF GREAT JOY: CHRISTMAS

The Gospel passages which narrate the events surrounding the birth and infancy of Jesus are found in the first chapters of the Gospels of St. Matthew and St. Luke. A guide to our reading of the infancy narratives as well as telling them to children, is this threefold theme that recurs throughout them all:

- "Do not be afraid";
- for "the Lord is near";
- therefore "Rejoice!"

Why? Because they announce the wonderful message of the Incarnation.

THE MYSTERY OF LOVE

The Incarnation is the moment in history when heaven and earth touch and merge together in the person of the Child. To help children to enter into this mystery of love, the Gospel texts which tell of the events before and after Christ's birth will offer us the key we need.

PRESENTING THE CHRISTMAS
MYSTERY TO THE CHILDREN

In telling and reflecting on the infancy narratives with children, the following are the passages in Scripture we present to young children:

- the announcement of Christ's Incarnation/the annunciation to Mary the Mother of God
  (Gospel of Luke, Chapter 1, verses 26—38);
- the visitation of Mary to Elizabeth
  (Gospel of St. Luke, Chapter 1, verses 39–49; 56);
- the birth of Jesus and the adoration of the Shepherds

(Gospel of St. Luke, Chapter 2, verses 1–20);

- the adoration of the three kings or Magi
  (Gospel of St. Matthew, Chapter 2, verses 1–12);
- the presentation of Jesus in the temple
  (Gospel of St. Luke, Chapter 2, verses 21–33; 36–39).

In reflecting on these, we guide the children to discover two elements which appear to be in direct contrast:

- the birth of this Child belongs to the everyday sphere of life;
- at the same time, this event belongs to a different and unique level of reality.

This is the heart of the mystery of the Incarnation: two worlds come together and become fused together in the Child of Bethlehem. The "sign" in which we see the immeasurable greatness of the "Son of the Most High" is a Child (Luke 2:12).

LISTENING AND REFLECTING WITH THE CHILDREN

A few general guidelines in presenting children the events associated with Christmas are:

- as with every other "sign" the child needs help to read and reflect on its message;
- the time of listening together, this meditative approach helps the children to enter into its meaning;
- and this special sign is the *Child*!
- thus, as with the other scripture texts of the parables, help the children to understand that there is a secret to discover, a marvel to wonder at, a mystery to unfold in which we have a part too.
- each of these events has its own moment; they are separated into single episodes so that the children may savor the glad tidings of each (the Annunciation of Gabriel to Mary, the visit of Mary to Elizabeth, the birth of Jesus, and the adoration of the shepherds and the Magi, the presentation in the Temple).
- use the actual words of Scripture. Since we are dealing with historical events whose scope is so great that we can hardly grasp it ourselves, stay as close as possible to the words of the Gospel;
- the Gospel offers us the language we need to help communicate the great significance of the event of Christ's birth and to help the children become aware of its significance in their lives.

PRESENTING THE NATIVITY NARRATIVE
TO THE CHILD(REN)

To give some specific indications of the sequence of presenting historical passages in the Bible, this brief outline of the Nativity is offered as an example.

TELLING THE EVENT

Narrate the Scripture passage to children, telling in your own words the birth of Christ, while using the actual words of the Gospel.

PROCLAIMING GOD'S WORD

Read the Gospel text slowly, perhaps using candles to contribute to the solemn atmosphere.

PRESENTING THE MATERIALS

The materials for the infancy narratives are presented at this point. Use your Christmas creche, if you have one; the figures should be three dimensional if possible (as most creche sets are) and they should be movable rather than pasted in place (as some crib sets can be).

Indicate the pieces and figures briefly:

"This is (to represent) the place where Jesus was born in Bethlehem"

(Put out the piece representing the stable or cave at Bethlehem).

"This is (to represent) Mary"

(Place the figure of Mary in the creche/stable set).

"This is (to represent) Joseph"

(Place out the figure of Joseph in the creche/stable set).

"And this is (to represent) the child Jesus"

(Place out the figure of Christ).

Once the figures are set out (which the children are usually familiar with), gently guide the children to reflect on what this could mean for us. This allows the children to ponder the deeper, personal meaning for them of this event.

LISTENING AND REFLECTING WITH THE CHILD(REN)

To do this, it helps to highlight these two elements: the ordinary and the extraordinary. Reflect and meditate with the child(ren) on this twofold dimension of the birth of Christ, so that they are struck by the sense of mystery.

A few of the guiding points in reflection together with the children are:

- Christmas celebrates the birth of a child;
- a child who was the same as we all were as children;
- Jesus was a child who needed his parents for everything, just as we did;
- a child who was "wrapped in bands of cloth," just like every baby at that time was.

And yet:

- this Child is called the "Son of the Most High";
- to him belongs a "throne";
- because "He will rule";
- His birth "will be a joy for all nations";
- this Child, named Jesus, is "Christ the Lord."

Using the language of the Bible in this way, and drawing the children to see the grandeur of this event, opens the door to wonder in their heart. This great event is not simply something that happened in the distant past, merely a part of ancient history. The children are helped to enter into this event here and now. Together we ask ourselves, in amazement, "But who can this Child be?" Stressing the greatness of the Incarnation in this way makes it easier for children to catch hold of its eternal presence in their own lives.

EASTER

The season of Easter offers us the opportunity to share with children the greatest Good News of all, the Lord is Risen! The seven weeks when the Church celebrates the feast of Easter, is the time to concentrate on proclaiming the resurrection to children and to help them experience the powerful impact it conveys.

To give two examples of a way of doing this, we will indicate: 1) how to present a Gospel text of the resurrection to children; 2) how to tell children about the Liturgy of the Light during the Easter Vigil celebration. However, every theme of the Christian message we present to children is rooted in and refers back to the resurrection, especially Baptism and the Eucharist. Nonetheless, the resurrection is not something we take for granted with the children; in fact, we announce it boldly in big letters.

The resurrection cannot be over-emphasized with children. Unfortunately it is often the passion and death of Jesus which is stressed; this can evoke feelings of anguish, especially in little children. Instead, we need to open the doors of hope for them.

ANNOUNCING THE RESURRECTION

Proclaiming the Christian message to children does not mean stressing Christ's suffering and death, but rather, that by passing through suffering and death, Christ came to the resurrection. Christ is risen. Death no longer has any power over Christ; death has been conquered forever. This is why the faith of a Christian is faith in goodness which is stronger than evil; it is faith in life, which is stronger than death.

In speaking about the resurrection with children, we are invited to make the words of the prophet Isaiah our own: to go up to "a high mountain" so that the message of the resurrection can reach as far as possible and to lift up our voices (Isaiah 40:9) so that as many children as possible can hear the good tidings, "Christ is Risen."

I. PRESENTING THE RESURRECTION TO THE CHILD(REN)

The focal point in narrating the events surrounding Christ's resurrection is to proclaim to children, again and again:

- that death does not have the last word in our destiny as human creatures;
- that there is Someone in our midst who has conquered death forever;
- and whose victory will become our victory.

Listening and reflecting on this great event with children follows the guidelines outlined in reference to the other historical events in the life of Christ. As an example, we will address what happened with Mary of Magdalene and the other women who went to the place where Christ was buried.

TELLING THE EVENT

- Tell the children the account of the happenings surrounding the resurrection of Christ.
- Remain close to the actual words of Scripture.
- Narrate in your own words the events that took place, following the Gospel account carefully.

READING GOD'S WORD

Then, as with each biblical passage we present to the children, read the text solemnly, using lighted candles to symbolize the presence of God in the Word.

LISTENING AND REFLECTING TOGETHER WITH THE CHILD(REN)

The meditation begins by reflecting on the "empty tomb." Centering on this theme, we ponder together the meaning of the words: "Why do you look for the living among the dead? He is not here, but has risen" (Luke 24:5).

In reflecting with the children, start by noting the amazement of the women who were the first witnesses to the resurrection:

- they go to the tomb brokenhearted; they are planning to perform the final preparations of the body for burial.

- But when they get there they find the tomb is open and empty! (Mark 16:4).

- They are so surprised; but their dismay grows even greater when they see a person of dazzling light (Matthew 28:3).

- They are seeing the Risen One himself. Mary Magdalene recognizes him when he calls her by name (John 20:16).

- And the wonder we feel ourselves—now, almost two thousand years from that Sunday's dawn—is something like the amazement those women felt.

- A new quality of life has come into the world. The life of the Risen Christ.

- This risen life is all life, in which death is a thing of the past.

II. THE LITURGY OF THE LIGHT

One characteristic of the religious experience we share with children is the quality of celebration; what we do with young children is approached in and leads to the spirit of celebration. The Liturgy of the Light, in relation to the proclamation of the resurrection with children, is an example of this.

What is proclaimed in the Bible is lived in the liturgy. Helping children to experience this reality (as we found with the Good Shepherd parable and the Mass), offers them an opportunity to enjoy more fully the relationship they have with God and others. This is especially true in the Liturgy of the Light, an important part of the Easter Vigil. It is one of the experiences that remain vividly clear in the children's memory, even when they become adults.

CELEBRATING THE LITURGY OF THE LIGHT WITH CHILDREN

Young children can be helped to participate in the celebration of the Liturgy of the Light, by highlighting its various elements. This enables the children to have an active role in the celebration and also prepares them to appreciate more fully this part of the Easter Vigil liturgy. Some of the major parts of the Liturgy of the Light to point out to and celebrate with children are:

- On the eve of Easter, when the church is in darkness, the paschal candle is lighted. It overpowers the darkness at a single stroke.

- With this one flame the procession goes forward towards the altar.

- When this single light of the paschal candle is lit, these words are said (or sung): "Christ our light."

- It is that light alone which guides us and makes it possible to walk forward. Without it we could not even see.

- This is the (symbol of the) light of the Risen Christ.

- The Risen Christ does not keep this new light, which was enkindled in the world at the moment of his resurrection, all to himself. He gives it to each one of us.

- During the celebration we see this light given to others, spreading to all the candles of the people gathered there, flooding the surroundings with light.

- And this light comes to us too.

After this kind of narration, the children are invited to light their own candles from the paschal candle. The children are carefully prepared to hold and carry their own personal candles. For instance:

- show the children how to hold the candle safely;

- show the children how to carry the lighted candle by shielding the flame—that precious light!—with their hand.

When children are prepared in this way, you may have confidence in their abilities.

The language of signs is powerful and requires little explanation. It is enough to help young children to use all their physical senses to enter into the meaning of what is happening. At the Easter Vigil there is something for every sense:

- the aroma of the incense;

- the resounding singing of the "Alleluia!";

- the ringing of the bells;

- the warmth of the candle's flame;

- the touch of the soft wax.

What a richness of signs there is for children to experience.

In the cathedral in Chihuahua, Mexico, 400 children celebrated the Liturgy of the Light (without the least incident). There was only one surprise. At the moment when the paschal candle was lighted, all the children began to applaud. This was totally spontaneous and unexpected. The applause, their way of welcoming and greeting the Light, lasted for several minutes!

11. PRAYER

It is from praying with children that we have learned most about the difference between the religious worlds of the child and the adult. If there is one dimension of the child's relationship with God that has taught us the need for respect and reverence, it is this aspect of prayer.

THE CHILD'S PRAYER

We have found that it requires an attentive attitude on our part if we are to help children pray in a way that responds to their needs and capacities. When we began to watch and listen to how young children pray, we noticed immediately a great difference between their prayer and ours.

The prayer of young children is composed essentially of praise and thanksgiving:

> Thank you God, for you.
> Thank you Father, for me.
> Thank you God for the light.

Their prayer of thanksgiving focuses on the many gifts God gives us: two children pray together:

> Thank you for coming into our hearts,
> because now we can pray to you inside us.
>
> [The other child adds.] Yes, he's really a great friend,
> and we will never be
> alone.

At times praise and thanksgiving are brought together:

> Thank you for making bread.
> Thank you for the light.
> Jesus, you are a treasure.

Other times, prayer and meditation are combined:

> Jesus gives us a hand of love
> so that we can rise again.

Children will use various kinds of comparisons:

> Jesus, you are a tree
> that lasts forever....
>
> Jesus you are like the moon.
> At night we can't see anything
> without the moon. Without you
> everything is dark.

In the Bible we find the blessing or benediction form of prayer: Jesus prays "I thank you Father..." (Matthew 11:25), and Mary, "My soul magnifies the Lord" (Luke 1:47). It is an expression of joy and adoration, a prayer born of wonder, which keeps our eyes turned towards the face of God. In listening to young children we hear an echo of this type of biblical prayer.

Little children tend to pray with few words. A young child prays before the Christmas crib, "Alleluia to the mighty God." Although the child prays with few words, this does not mean the child prays only for a short time. The inner attitude of the child's prayer lasts a long time.

For instance, in praying with a group of children there are often intervals of silence between the prayer of one child and another. So it happened with this prayer (we mention only the last part here) where there were spaces of silence which lasted quite a while:

> Thank you for leading us...
>
> Thank you because we are
> your sheep...
>
> Thank you for coming
> into our hearts...
>
> My body is happy.

During the silence between the prayers of one child and the next, the group of children remained in an attitude of quiet recollection.

These moments of silence are prayer as well: "Silence is praise to you, O God" (Psalm 65:1). These spaces of silence—precious, rich moments working like yeast in the child's spirit—reflect the child's rhythm of doing things. Becoming attuned to this helps us to respect these wordless intervals in the prayer of young children. Rather than interrupting the flow of prayer by thinking the silence means the child is distracted by other things, we become aware that these too are moments of the child's union with God.

THE QUALITY OF PRAYER

We have been able to collect so very little of the prayer of young children.[1] Who can tell how many mysteries are still unknown to us, when prayer occurs in the solitary, hidden place of the child's heart? When her mother wanted to pray with her, three year old Ana Sofia responded, "I pray alone...."

Children will sometimes express the aspect of offering in their prayer:

> I give you my whole world,
> which is my heart.
>
> Everything that is most
> beautiful in the world,
> I give to you.

Yet the basic quality in the young child's prayer remains praise and gratitude. Children embrace a wide assortment of things relating to various levels of life. There is thanksgiving for:

> a mouth to eat with
> hands for touching
> legs to walk and play football

> for: an aunt
>   "grandparents, brothers,
>   parents, little cousins, parables"

---

[1] See *The Religious Potential of the Child* by Sofia Cavalletti, Chapter Seven.

"school for studying and learning
so many things"

for: "medicines for healing"
        "the beautiful sky
        and beautiful stars"
        "the sea, little birds,
        and all beautiful things"

for: "I thank you for making
        us live and letting us
        play with our friends"

        "I thank you because
        you opened the doors
        of my heart."

On the other hand, prayers of petition are extremely rare in the prayer of young children. It appears that asking for things is not the form of prayer which comes naturally to them. It seems to us that children have their own path in prayer, one that corresponds to what is actually within them. We have learned not to direct them to petition prayers in case it may become merely a repetition of words without any deep, inner attachment in their own hearts.

HELPING THE CHILD'S PRAYER

Faced with this situation, what do we do to help the child's prayer?

First, the primary concern is helping the child's prayer, rather than teaching prayers to children. Our hope is to help children enter into prayer: that inner disposition by which the heart turns to God in openness so as to listen and respond to the presence of Love.

ONLY ONE TEACHER

In order to do this we asked ourselves: Do we want to make children pray or are we willing to pray *with* children? The first way puts us in the position of *the* teacher and separates our prayer from the child's. The second way invites us to be together with children in the presence of the mystery of the infinite God. What a discovery this was! In trying to be with children in this way we came to the awareness that children reach a depth of knowing and feeling in their relationship with God that is far beyond anything we have been able to offer.

In being with children we have at times sensed a mysterious and silent presence which does not belong to us. At times like this we recognize there is only one teacher, the inner Teacher. God alone teaches the children, and us too.

The children teach as well. In praying together with children and hearing their words, the adult's prayer moves into the realm of praise and thanksgiving, which may be often neglected in our inner life. Being attentive to the way young children express prayer can be valuable for us because they help us to learn or re-learn how to open ourselves to the aspect of *enjoyment* in our relationship with God. How important this is in the religious life of each one of us. What a gift it is to be helped to regain it.

PRAYER AS LISTENING

Before being a response on our part, prayer is first a listening to and being aware of God's presence in our lives. We can nourish children's prayer by helping them to know God. And we do this especially by proclaiming what God has let us know about himself, by telling the mighty works God has done for us.

This proclamation of the Christian message is the starting point for prayer. How could we respond to God, if God had not first spoken to us? When we offer children this message of glad tidings and communicate it in a living way, children take hold of it with joy and wonder and their response is warm and deep.

Telling children about God's great gestures of love in our human history offers them a rich source and stimulus for prayer.

PROCLAIMING GOD'S LOVE

Introducing children to the Bible and liturgy gives them a language for prayer.

In the various prayers mentioned in this chapter, you can hear the echoes of the themes we have been reflecting on together, such as the parables of the kingdom of God and the sacraments that are presented to children.

The following are a few examples of how to offer children a language for prayer:

- Tell the children some of the biblical names for God. For instance, during the weeks of Advent, speak about the thousands of years of waiting the people of God lived through. With what longing did they desire the coming of the Child who, as the prophet proclaims, is:

> Wonderful Counselor,
> Mighty God,
> Eternal Father,
> Prince of Peace.
> (Isaiah 9:6)

Knowing that Jesus is called by names like these helps children enter into the spirit of prayer and gives them a rich vocabulary for prayer.

- Psalms are another example of the biblical language that nurtures the child's prayer. For instance, after they have come to know about the Good Shepherd through the Gospel parables, introduce them to the psalm that begins: "The Lord is my shepherd" (Psalm 23). This is done very gradually, almost line by line, over a long period of time. We cannot hurry so precious a reality as prayer.

- Print out (in a decorative way) a line of this psalm or others such as "The Lord is my light," (Psalm 27) and place in the area or on the table set aside for prayer. The children may trace and color it, or copy it in their own hand if they are able.

PRAYERS

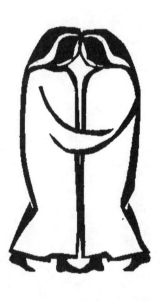

When it comes to established prayer forms, there are two guidelines that are helpful.

- The first approach to introducing children to traditional prayers relates to the aspect of prayer as listening. For example, when speaking with the child(ren) on the greeting of Gabriel to Mary (Luke 1:28), you are also offering an introduction to the first part of a cherished prayer. Later, recall this Gospel passage and with this biblical context as the foundation, give only the first few words of the prayer: "Hail Mary full of grace."

Another example is the account of Mary's visit to Elizabeth in the same Gospel. Filled with joy, Elizabeth welcomes Mary with words inspired by the presence of the Holy Spirit, "Blessed are you among women" (Luke 1:42). At a later time, you may reflect on this prayer phrase as well with the child(ren) and these words will strike an inner chord because the biblical account is known already through listening to it.

■ The second, implied in the first, is to follow the child's natural way of praying by using very short phrases of prayers or even single words. For instance, reflect with the child(ren) on the one-word prayer response "Amen" (and link it to what they are already familiar with, such as the great "Amen" which follows the gesture of offering in the Mass) or "Alleluia." This helps the child develop that inner agility whereby prayer is a genuine and spontaneous expression.

Though long prayer formulas seem to contrast with young children's own way of prayer, there comes a time when they are ready. In the same way as before, begin with only a few words at a time. For example, offer the words,

> "Our Father who art in heaven";

later, add

> "Hallowed be thy name,"

and later another phrase,

> "thy kingdom come,"

and so forth, phrase by phrase, over a period of time.

TIME FOR PRAYER

As for the different times for prayer, recalling the child to pray on a regular basis throughout the day is a useful support so that prayer is not forgotten or overlooked in day to day life.

Parents and those of you who are in daily contact with children can help them exercise that inner movement of the heart—which is the spirit of prayer—in relation to the events of everyday life, such as at meal times and before bedtime, and so forth. There are many opportunities to pray together with the child; some joy, a particular happening, or whatever is part of the child's ordinary life can present an occasion for prayer. This helps the child to understand that prayer is not only for certain times or places.

CREATING SILENCE

Silence is an essential element in helping children's prayer. By this is meant more than the silence that occurs during the moment of prayer itself; we mean silence as an important dynamic in the religious formation of children.

Many of us find it very difficult to believe how much young children enjoy silence. As the time of her first Communion drew near, a child wrote: "I like everything here, but silence is the thing I like best." In fact, silence is something the child searches for and loves. There is a quality of silence in which the child feels completely at home.

The more children live in the midst of confusion, the more they need silence, just as people who live in places where the air is polluted need pure, fresh air. Yet, even the atmosphere of noise and confusion that usually surrounds children in our modern age does not manage to destroy their need for silence and for the many values connected with it.

The silence the child seeks is not the kind that is imposed from the outside (as in a class when children are all asked to be quiet, for instance). Instead, the quality of silence we have seen in young children is something that arises from within them, bringing a restful stillness to the body and a spirit of recollection to the heart. The young child is searching for an interior silence.

To create a climate of silence is a way of helping the child's inner meditative spirit. Creating time and space for silence is a way of nourishing that special need for listening which is at the heart of the child's prayer. Silence becomes the soil in which the child's prayer may flourish and grow.

12. MORAL FORMATION

In coming to the close of the book, we would like to address a final question: What about the child's moral formation? Is it possible to speak in terms of moral formation with respect to young children under six or seven years of age? The answer to this question depends on what is meant by the word "moral."

If the meaning of the term "moral" is restricted to laws and codes of behavior, then any detailed discussion should be postponed until after age six. Around six years of age or so a new and vital need is born in children which leads them to concrete concerns about what is fair or unfair, good or bad, should or should not be done. However, moral formation has a much deeper meaning, one that goes far beyond rules and standards of behavior.

TWO LEVELS: BEING AND DOING

There are two levels to keep in mind in speaking about moral formation. The first level is the formation of the person; this is the foundation. Each of us is formed through the dynamic of relationships. Each of us needs to be in relationship with others and it is in the relationship with others that our own person is being formed. This shows how vital it is for the child to find the right partner with whom to create such a relationship.

In moral formation, the first level engages all the aspects of our life, our whole person. This is the level at which we acquire our fundamental attitude or *orientation* towards life. This orientation takes hold at the very roots of our being.

The second is the level of *behavior* or actions; it derives and takes its life from the first. The second level—behavior—differs from the first level—the foundation—in that there is one basic orientation in our life whereas there are many actions or ways of behaving.

The first, orientation, is rooted in the level of being, the second, behavior, in the level of doing. But the second takes its value from the first because it is *who* we are that gives value to *what* we do.

The image of the chandelier may help to illustrate these two different levels. The chandelier can be compared to the person, and its many lights to actions. The bulbs of the chandelier light up only when the chandelier is connected to its energy or power source. So too for us. It is the orientation of our life that illuminates all our actions. This is another reason why early childhood is such a crucial period, because when concerns on the level of behavior emerge around the age of six, it is important that the children are already oriented in a certain way in life, and that they already have established relationships with others.

THE COVENANT RELATIONSHIP

The perspective highlights the significance of the child's relationships with parents and others, and with the environment. There is another fundamental relationship in the life of the human person: the relationship with God. God's relationship with us is rooted at a far deeper level than the intellectual plane alone; this relationship is already present from the earliest part of our lives.

All the major themes of the Christian message outlined in this book have one aim: to help children discover and enjoy the presence of Someone in their lives. There is a Person who calls them by name, who creates the most steadfast and enduring relationship of love; it is Someone who, in giving them the gift of his own life and his own "light," gives them his whole self.

FALLING IN LOVE WITH GOD

We try to help little children to become conscious of and attentive to the voice that is calling them by name. This voice calls them to *be* before it calls them to *do*. Put in biblical language, our aim is to help children become aware of the God of the covenant, of the God who is searching for us. God is searching for us because he loves us.

We try to help little children discover in wonderment the presence of a light that was given to us as a gift, of a mysterious and powerful seed within them which grows and leads towards more life, life in its fullness. This seed is so beautiful and valuable that it can be compared to the precious pearl of great price. And all of this has been given to us as a gift.

In contemplating these realities, the relationship with God is created and it is established on the foundation of enjoying God's presence. Childhood is the time for the peaceful and serene enjoyment of God, the time for being in love. Being in love is the essential foundation for the child's moral life.

A time will come for effort, struggle, and even sacrifice. There will come a time when we must teach children the standards of the Christian life as well. Yet "for everything there is a season," says Ecclesiastes (3:1-8).

BEING IN LOVE

Therefore, try not to disturb the child's encounter with God with untimely preoccupations about results on the level of *doing*. Instead, if what we offer the young child is free from exhortations about doing or not doing certain things, it will have an even greater effect on the formation of the child's whole person. This means we are feeding that inner wellspring, the source from which the child's behavior will flow forth in later childhood.

Our call is to help young children become conscious of a certain reality, and to experience and enjoy it. When the child falls in love, then it will blossom anew in later childhood and color the moral concerns of this period with its light, the light of love.

Religious formation in early childhood should be free from worries about quick immediate results on a practical level and from concerns about influencing the child's future behavior. On a practical level, early childhood is the time to help children open themselves to the *enjoyment* of God's presence in their lives. Religious education should be primarily educating the child to enjoy the relationship with God with deep awareness and great wonder.

That being said, however, we have seen that when themes are presented in this way to young children, they later become points of reference for the new life experiences the child begins to live (after the age of six). In early childhood, the little child contemplates and is captivated by these themes. In later childhood, these same realities are touched and activated once again, and become the mainspring for the older child's behavior.

This affirms that the Christian message given in early childhood truly represents a vital, life-giving experience for children. Their contemplation of the satisfying reality of God's protective love and their awareness that the Good Shepherd calls each "by name" is a fruitful experience in their lives. Its effect is so deep that children can spontaneously recall and draw on it *even years later*.

In conclusion then, the themes that have been outlined become deeply implanted in the lives of children. Children are able to apply them to different life situations as they grow older.

Thus, the children have not only experienced the certainty of being loved but they also have received a seed. This seed is capable of bearing immediate fruit in their lives—the most wonderful fruit of all—the enjoyment of God's presence. This same seed is capable of bearing long-range fruit. The experience of being in love nourishes and strengthens the child's inner life for the future as well.

APPENDICES

APPENDICES

APPENDIX A: THE CATECHESIS OF THE GOOD SHEPHERD

What has been described in this book is based on an approach to the religious formation of children, commonly referred to as the Catechesis of the Good Shepherd. This Appendix offers a brief introduction to this approach that has been developing for many years, and provides a context in which to view the Appendix that follows.

The Catechesis of the Good Shepherd had a mustard seed beginning. The soil it found was in the meeting of two persons, Sofia Cavalletti and Gianna Gobbi. It is more than their story, since the seed and its growth belong to God and many others had a hand in its sowing. It is told here simply as background for your reading of the following program for children and guidelines for catechists (Appendix B).

Sofia's path seemed directed towards an university career. Proficient in languages, modern and ancient, she obtained her doctorate in Hebrew and Semitic languages, with a diploma of specialization in Philology and Semitic culture and history.

This choice of studies was determined partly by Dr. Eugenio Zolli, Sofia's first Hebrew teacher during her undergraduate days. His coming into the Catholic Church (recorded in his autobiography *Before the Dawn*, Sheed and Ward), combined with his Judaic roots (he had been the chief rabbi of Rome until 1945), were formative factors both in their friendship and studies that followed. Hebrew scholarship became a shared work, continuing up to the time of Zolli's death. It has occupied an important position in Sofia's life ever since: with contributions to various editions of the Bible, translating and annotating original biblical texts, and extensive writings on post-biblical Hebraic tradition and ecumenical matters. In later years she was to receive appointments to various ecumenical committees, including the Vatican commission on Jewish-Christian relations and the Italian Ecumenical Commission, the first of its kind to invite lay members to participate in the Italian Episcopal Conference.

Gianna also had a mentor who was to affect the direction of her life, Dr. Maria Montessori, Italy's famous educator of children. While still in her teens, Gianna had already started her apprenticeship in Montessori's approach to education. Her studies led her to choose early childhood education as her basis, working with children as young as two years of age.

In 1951, after many years' experience with children and one year before Dr. Montessori's death, Gianna was invited to assist Montessori in her teacher training course. Her involvement in the training of teachers continued; by 1960 this included the specialized work of forming adults to care for children from birth to three years of age ("Assistants to Infancy"). Eventually Gianna's work in this field would extend beyond Italy, leading her to direct adult formation courses in Mexico and in the United States.

This information is not intended to center attention on Sofia and Gianna and their respective fields of expertise. Instead, their attitude is that the message matters most, not the messengers; their conviction is that the adult's presence in God's relationship with the child is as an "unprofitable servant" (Luke 17:10). Being part of this mystery would become a source of wonder and being close to children would always have the impact of gift. So much so that, thirty-five years afterwards, they would write in a letter to their Canadian co-workers:

> It happens that in being with children we will sense the presence of a force, mysterious and silent, which does not belong to us, and we will treasure it as an inestimable privilege to be granted at times to "see" it working within the child. As Elijah did, on Mount Horeb, when he heard the "tiny, whispering sound," at moments like this we too will want to "cover our face" in beholding the presence of God (1 Kings 19:13).[1]

Nonetheless, their backgrounds do indicate two pillars underpinning the Catechesis of the Good Shepherd. One is the strong theological foundation, with its reverence for the Bible and the liturgy as direct sources of God's self-communication to us. The other is the solid pedagogical foundation, with its respect for the person and the potential of the child. The first rests on the belief that God, who is Love, seeks to love us and for our love, and that the human heart hungers to receive and return this love. The second pillar rests on the belief that since God's love is unconditional, including the condition of chronological age, even the very young child is invited into this covenant relationship.

It is true, then, that their backgrounds do indicate these foundations. Yet this does not account for what was to follow as an outgrowth. When their paths came together, the unexpected was awaiting them. They were to see for themselves that God not only communicates with the young child, but that in the child God finds a partner especially responsive to the overture of love. No less surprising, they discovered that young children are not only able to enter into this relationship, but that they have a special capacity to experience and enjoy the presence of God.

To return to the sequence of our story, their meeting was due to a mutual friend, Adele Costa Gnocchi (herself a well-known Montessorian), who saw in Sofia and Gianna something which perhaps neither was aware of in themselves. Maybe Adele knew that each had experiences which appeared to ready them, indirectly, for what was soon to follow. Gianna's years of day-to-day presence to children brought her to the realization that the child truly is made in the image of God. This awareness was transformative: "I was born in the child," as she expresses it. For Sofia it was a single incident that sounded a deep chord within. A friend, who had a six-year-old son, asked Sofia if she would give him some help in the religious sphere. Without any teaching aids or experience with children, she agreed at least to meet with him. When they did, she opened the Bible to the first page and together they began listening to the Word and speaking about it. The child's response was altogether unexpected; even after two hours he was still happy to be there. "Why," she reflected afterwards, "is he so happy?" In each of their lives, it appears, the ground was prepared for something more.

It was at this point that they met. Adele was instrumental in God's "plan" of love (Ephesians 1:9ff.) for it was she who sent Gianna and Sofia their first group of children. In accepting her invitation they had set foot in the direction of what was to become—unknown to them—a lifetime dedication. However, at that time they were aware only of their own seeming limitations. But in welcoming those first four children they had been touched by joy: "If our work did not end after a brief number of meetings, as we planned, we owe it to the response, full of enthusiasm, solemn joy, serenity and depth of these four children."

So it was that, in the springtime of 1954, the Good Shepherd Formation Centre, as it is called today, came to be born.

How to serve the religious needs of young children? Drawing on Montessori's experiments in the field of religious education,[2] they arranged an atrium for them. This environment was

---

[1] "And a little child shall lead them...". Trans. Patricia Coulter. The Catechesis of The Good Shepherd *Newsletter, Number 7* (English) Winter 1990, p. 6. (Contact: The Catechesis of the Good Shepherd, Box 1084, Oak Park, IL 60304, for inquiries about the Newsletter.)

[2] See Maria Montessori, *The Child In The Church*, E. M. Standing, ed. (St. Paul: Catechetical Guild, 1965).

prepared with furnishings and activities adapted to young children, in order to allow them to be and do in their own way and rhythm. Gradually other rooms were prepared for children six to twelve years of age as well and arranged according to their developmental needs.

Another challenge had to be faced: How could the Christian message be communicated so that even the very young child could hear and receive it? Once again they benefitted from Montessori's insights, knowing that, if the child was to be helped to approach and experience the presence of God, the message had to be materialized, so to speak, in some concrete form. Therefore they set about making materials which would provide the child with a first-hand, personal contact with the heart of Christian revelation. By involving the use of the children's senses and offering them opportunities for movement, the materials served as tangible instruments for the child's encounter with God. In fact, in the child's hands they take on something of the quality of a "sacramental," according to an Italian moral theologian who has been long involved in the catechesis.[3]

Gradually a series of catechetical materials was developed. It was the children who guided this process. Through careful observation of their reactions, it was seen that some biblical or liturgical theme would draw forth a peaceful attitude in the child and an interest in using a certain material again and again. When a theme or material evoked this quality of response, they knew a vital need had been nurtured in the child. When a material proved its value to engage the child's desire and ability for prayer and meditation it was kept, otherwise it was discarded. To this day, this process continues.

As time went on, they realized that the themes that most nourished the child also happened to be the most crucial to the Christian message. The children did more than direct the selection process; they actually guided them to the choice of the essential elements of revelation. Only what is essential to the heart of the mystery appeared to satisfy the child's hunger, as, for instance, in the parable of the Good Shepherd. As Sofia suggests in the first chapter of this work, because of the deep resonance it called forth in them, it was the children who chose the Good Shepherd parable. Their choice echoes that of the first Christians, as can be seen in the catacombs of Rome. There it is the image of Jesus as the Good Shepherd which is the most prevalent of all the symbolic representations used to depict Christ.

During these experimental years, a growing community of adults gathered around the children. In 1963, they joined together with others, such as Dr. Silvana Montanaro, to found an association dedicated to serving the religious formation of the child.[4] It soon started becoming an international network, linking children and adults from many countries.

This created enduring bonds and opened avenues of communication among different cultures and traditions. By 1975 the seed had spread to North America, with a series of adult seminars—directed to the formation of catechists—following in rapid succession in the United States, Mexico and Canada. This new growth offered rich possibilities for dialogue. One example of this took place during their visit to Mexico. Up to that point this catechetical approach as yet had no name. During a conversation with a Mexican bishop, he referred to this work as the "Catechesis of the Good Shepherd," the name it has been known by ever since.

The catechesis began to take root in these and other countries such as Argentina and Colombia, in a variety of home, parish and school settings. Thus, an invaluable testing ground had appeared on an international scale. In exchanging experiences, it was found that certain themes of the Christian message evoked the same positive response in children of similar age, regardless of their cultural or class background. What emerged then was a nucleus of core themes, and it is these that are outlined in the following section.

---

[3] P. Dalmazio Mongillo, O.P. "Preface" to the Italian Edition of *Religious Potential*. Trans. Patricia Coulter. (*Newsletter, Number One*, p. 17-20).

[4] "Associazione Maria Montessori Per La Formazione Religiosa Del Bambino."

APPENDIX B: NOTES FOR CATECHISTS AND CURRICULUM FOR CHILDREN

NOTES FOR CATECHISTS

- As catechists we are called to unite ourselves to the child in listening together to the Word of God and in reflecting and meditating together with the child on the Word of God.

- As a way of predisposing ourselves for this, it is necessary to meditate on the theme before presenting it to children, and to practice using the materials (in whatever form we have available to us) before presenting them to children.

- It helps to keep a journal to record the presentations (especially to be able to offer individual help to any child absent from a session) and the child(ren)'s responses to them.

- It is important to have a celebration of the Eucharist, especially around Eastertime and, if possible, also at the end of the year. The celebrant should understand the needs of children so as to help them really live the Mass.

- The youngest children are invited to join in the Eucharistic celebration at the time of the preparation of the gifts. They can participate in the preparation of the gifts and in the procession of the gifts (particularly the cruets, which they themselves can fill with water and wine beforehand).

- It is not advisable to begin the catechetical year with the celebration of the Eucharist. The Mass is celebrated when a special atmosphere has been created and when the little children have begun to know about the meaning of the Eucharist.

CURRICULUM OUTLINE FOR CHILDREN

The following is an outline of the presentation of themes for young children arranged according to the seasons in the liturgical year. The outline is intended only as an orientation or indication to help you arrange your calendar with the children. It developed from and is based on the religious capacities of the child. Therefore, the *actual curriculum*—the sequence and timing of presenting the various themes of the Christian message—*depends on the individual child and the nature of the group of children.*

INTRODUCTION

- Three-year-old children should be introduced very gradually into the catechetical setting (which we call the *atrium*), preferably before the end of the liturgical year (September or October).

- As an approach to the themes outlined here, it is advisable to present the themes separated by a sufficient interval of time so that the children have the opportunity to enter into and to enjoy every aspect of the message.

- Each year certain themes are repeated, such as the proclamation of Christ's birth and resurrection. In keeping with the individual child's needs and the needs and capabilities of the group, new insights pertaining to the theme are offered each year and the children are thus helped to delve more deeply into these aspects of the Christian message year after year.

- A most important task of the catechist is to observe each child carefully. This enables the catechist to adapt the presentations and all the activities *to the child*, and to help the child's growth and personal interiorization of the Christian message.

- The catechist needs to have a knowledge of and great respect for the child's inner development, both in terms of the child's rhythm of entering into the message and the child's personal response to the Lord.

- The sequence and pace of presenting these themes depend on the developmental needs of the individual child and the particular group of children.

- The following program (see pages 95–98) offers an orientation for catechesis as presented to children from three to six years of age especially. We say *orientation* because it is intended as a guide (*not* to be applied in a fixed or rigid manner) in our service to God and the child together.

REMINDER TO OUR READERS

This outline is the fruit of the *children's choice* rather than the result of our own selection. Since the themes presented here were chosen on the basis of the children's response, we invite you to view what follows as a guideline or indication, rather than a structure to be followed rigidly. Since it is the child's relationship with God that is the center and heart of this catechesis, we invite you to approach and apply the following curriculum in this spirit.

TIME BEFORE ADVENT		
YEAR ONE	**YEAR TWO**	**YEAR THREE**
Introductory Meetings (four sessions): Introducing the children to the catechetical setting; various exercises to help the child(ren) to know and be comfortable in this setting	Introductory Meetings (two sessions): Familiarizing the child(ren) with the catechetical setting and recalling the routine for catechesis (various exercises)	Introductory Meetings (two sessions): Familiarizing the child(ren) with the catechetical setting and recalling the routine for catechesis (various exercises)
Small Altar: Altar, altar cloth, crucifix, chalice, paten, candles	Objects of the Mass: other articles associated with the Mass	Sign of the Cross: with meditation on the words; before the reading of the Gospel at Mass
Liturgical colors: The name of the vestment—chasuble	Vestments of the priest	The gesture of genuflection
		Objects of the Sanctuary: lamp, tabernacle, etc.
	Calendar of the Liturgical Year: the three major feasts	Calendar of the Liturgical Year: three major seasons in liturgical cycle

ADVENT AND CHRISTMAS

YEAR ONE	YEAR TWO	YEAR THREE
Advent Celebration: changing of cloth/ drape to purple; the four candles; new words—Advent and Christmas	Advent Celebration: changing of cloth/ drape to purple; meditation on the theme of Advent	Advent Celebration: changing of cloth/ drape to purple; meditation on the theme of Advent
Prophecies: the "Light" and the "Child" (Isaiah)	Prophets and Prophecies: the "Virgin" and "Bethlehem"	Prophets and Prophecies: the "Star" and synthesis
The world and the land of Jesus: globe of the earth-sensorial impression	Geography of the land of Jesus: 3 principal places—Nazareth, Bethlehem, Jerusalem, using topographical map and wooden map	Geography of the land of Jesus: places and features of the land of Israel, with map and related charts
The Annunciation: Introduction to "Hail Mary" prayer	The Visitation: The first part of the "Hail Mary"	Synthesis of the preceding accounts and the "Magnificat" prayer
The Birth of Jesus and the adoration of the shepherds	The Birth of Jesus and the adoration of the Magi	The Birth of Jesus
		Presentation of Jesus in the Temple
Celebration of Christmas: changing of cloth/ drape to white	Celebration of Christmas and Epiphany: changing of color to white	Celebration of Christmas and Epiphany: changing of color to white

SUNDAYS OF THE YEAR		
YEAR ONE	**YEAR TWO**	**YEAR THREE**
Celebration: changing of cloth to green	Celebration: changing of cloth to green	Celebration: changing of cloth to green
Parable of the mustard seed	Parable of the yeast/leaven	Parable of the seed (Mark 4:26–28)
Parable of the merchant and pearl	Parable of the hidden treasure	Celebration: the Kingdom of God

SEASON OF LENT		
YEAR ONE	**YEAR TWO**	**YEAR THREE**
Celebration: changing of cloth to purple; new words—Lent and Easter	Celebration: changing of cloth to purple; meditation on the theme of Lent	Celebration: changing of the cloth to purple; meditation on the theme of Lent
Parable of the Good Shepherd	Parable of the Found Sheep	The Eucharistic Presence of the Good Shepherd
Psalm of the Good Shepherd (verse 1)	Psalm of the Good Shepherd (verses 1–3)	Psalm of the Good Shepherd (verses 1–4)
The Cenacle: the Last Supper (to the Resurrection)	The Cenacle: the Last Supper (to the Apostles)	The Cenacle
Celebration of the Last Supper (only if there are older children in atrium)	Celebration of Last Supper	Celebration of Last Supper

SEASON OF EASTER		
YEAR ONE	**YEAR TWO**	**YEAR THREE**
Celebration: the Liturgy of Light; changing of cloth to white	Celebration: the Liturgy of Light; changing of cloth to white	Celebration: the Liturgy of Light; changing of cloth to white
Baptism: the light and the white garment	Map of Jerusalem: principal places	Map of Jerusalem: with names (cards)
Baptism: the water and the Word	Baptism: the gestures and the oils	The Grain of Wheat: the mystery of life and death.
The sign of the cross; the imposition of the hand		The cosmic cross
Preparation of the cruets (water and wine)	The mingling of the water and wine	The washing of the hands (lavabo)
Gesture of the Invocation of the Spirit (*epiclesis*)	Gesture of the offering	Gesture of the exchange of peace

PENTECOST		
YEAR ONE	**YEAR TWO**	**YEAR THREE**
Celebration of Pentecost: changing of cloth to red	Celebration of Pentecost: changing of cloth to red	Celebration of Pentecost: changing of cloth to red
The gifts of the Holy Spirit (7 red candles)	Meditation on the gifts of the Holy Spirit (names and 7 red candles)	Meditation and Reading of Pentecost account (7 red candles)

ABOUT THE AUTHORS

SOFIA CAVALLETTI

Sofia Cavalletti received her degree from the Università La Sapienza in Rome with a degree in Hebrew and Comparative Semitic Languages. She has contributed to several editions of the Bible (Old Testament,) translating Isaiah, Leviticus, Ruth, Esther, Judith and Proverbs, and to international publications on Biblical Studies. Dr. Cavalletti is also a specialist in the field of ecumenism, especially the Jewish-Christian relationship.

In 1954, Sofia Cavalletti founded, together with Gianna Gobbi, the Good Shepherd Centre of Catechesis for children and adults, which she continues to direct. Her work has spread through lectures, seminars, courses and publications in Canada, the U.S., Mexico, Colombia, Argentina and Germany. Dr. Cavalletti's book, *The Religious Potential of the Child* has been translated into English, Spanish and Portuguese.

PATRICIA COULTER

Toronto-born Patricia Coulter received the A.M.I. Diploma in Dublin, Ireland, after which she taught in Montessori children's centers in Ireland, the United States and Canada. She then pursued theological studies in Rome and studied for two years under the direction of Dr. Cavalletti and Prof. Gobbi for which she was granted the Catechetical Diploma from the Vicariate of Rome.

In 1978 Patricia Coulter received her religious education degree (M.R.E.) at the Toronto School of Theology and since then has been engaged in the religious formation of children and adults as well as establishing centers of catechesis in parish and school settings. In 1991, she was appointed Coordinator of the Catechesis of the Good Shepherd for the Archdiocese of Toronto and is also Director of the Certificate Programme in this catechesis, cosponsored by the University of St. Michael's College, University of Toronto and the Catholic Office of Religious Education, Archdiocese of Toronto.

GIANNA GOBBI

Gianna Gobbi began working with Dr. Maria Montessori in 1940 and in 1942 she assumed responsibility for the two-year-old children in the "Casa dei Bambini" (Children's House) of Prof. Adele Costa Gnocchi in Palazzo Taverna, Rome. Professor Gobbi collaborated as Dr. Montessori's Assistant during her course on young children in 1951. Since 1959 she has been offering lectures to adults caring for children under the age of three at the Assistants to Infancy

Training Program in Rome. In addition, she is also principal lecturer with Dr. Silvana Montanaro at the A.M.I. Assistants to Infancy Course in Houston, Texas and Rome, Italy.

Gianna Gobbi is co-founder of the Centre of Catechesis in Rome which specializes in catechesis with children from three to twelve years of age. Since 1954, she has been working with Sofia Cavalletti in the religious formation of children, and continues to co-direct the Centre with her as well as collaborating in adult catechetical training courses in Italy, and Toronto, Canada.

DR. SILVANA QUATTROCCHI MONTANARO

Dr. Silvana Quattrocchi Montanaro obtained her degree in Medicine and Surgery from the University of Rome, and specialized in psychiatry. She is a psychotherapist and an expert on the problems of the formative years. For many years she lectured on mental hygiene and neuro-psychiatry at the Scuola Assistenti all'Infanzia (Assistants to Infancy) in Rome, preparing adults to care for children under three years of age.

Dr. Quattrocchi Montanaro is a trainer of childbirth educators using the Respiratory Autogenic Training method and prepares prospective parents with RAT, lectures and discussions on educational problems of the first years of life. She currently directs the A.M.I. Assistants to Infancy course in Rome (Italy), Denver (U.S.A.), and London (England).